OUTSPOKEN ESSAYS
ON MUSIC

Outspoken Essays on Music

BY

CAMILLE SAINT-SAËNS
(*de l'Institut*)

AUTHORISED TRANSLATION BY
FRED ROTHWELL

..

With musical illustrations in the text.

GREENWOOD PRESS, PUBLISHERS
WESTPORT, CONNECTICUT

Originally published in 1922
by Kegan Paul, Trench, Trubner & Co., Ltd., London
and E. P. Dutton & Co., New York

Reprinted from an original copy in the collections
of the Brooklyn Public Library

First Greenwood Reprinting 1970

Library of Congress Catalogue Card Number 79-100835

SBN 8371-4010-2

Printed in the United States of America

CONTENTS

PART I

PART II

FOREWORD

"La Musique est dans tout, un Hymne sort du Monde,"
said Victor Hugo, who did not understand music, though
he felt intuitively the importance and beauty of that
vapeur de l'art which became condensed in wonder-
producing forms, as well as of those vapourous con-
densations of the atmosphere into splendid and glorious
clouds, the fabled abode of the thunderbolts fashioned
by the gods of old.

Primitive men, the higher they rose in the animal
scale of evolution, doubtless modulated their savage
cries and discovered . . . singing ! Curious to relate,
birds sing ; whereas the mammalia, for which so grand
a future was in store, do not sing. It was necessary
that man should appear on the stage of life before song
. . . and subsequently music . . . were forthcoming.
Music therefore is the most plastic, as well as the young-
est, of the arts. Why is this ? Because music applies to
two different arts based on *sound*, just as painting and
engraving have their one common origin in drawing.

" Primary " music, that which appeared simultaneously with the human race itself, consists of two elements : melody and rhythm. It held sway throughout
Europe up to the time of the Middle Ages and still reigns
throughout both the Near and the Far East. The

Greeks and nearer Orientals have varied and intensified
the usual modes and modulations of sound in their
melodies ; whereas rhythm, among the distant Oriental
nations has attained to a degree of perfection, a truly
extraordinary artistic complexity, that cannot be approached by our Western musicians.

Legends abound as regards the power of expression,
the truly superhuman results, obtained by this
" primary " music. Wild animals crawling at the feet
of Orpheus ; Saul's madness soothed and calmed by
the strains of David's harp ; the vocation or calling of
the Buddha determined by the vibrations of the strings
of a vina ; the passions of Alexander roused or lulled
at will by the various melodies drawn from a lyre, without speaking of walls erected by the music of Amphion's
lyre or dashed to the ground by the trumpets of the
Hebrews. Wide is our choice among the phenomena
of the marvellous, wherein the potency of the results
effected contrasts strangely with the poverty of the
means employed to bring them about.

Nor let us forget to mention the famous contest
between Apollo and Marsyas where we actually see
emphasised, on the one hand, the predilection of the
great ones of earth for trivial music and their unconcern
for great art which bores them, and on the other hand,
the terribly cruel vengeance of the god, the irritation
of artistes at their lack of success, as well as their fierce
jealousy. Both Grétry and Sebastian Bach have dealt
with this fable ; the grave German maëstro giving proof
of an imaginative fancy calculated to astonish those
unacquainted with any but his serious productions :
while King Midas is speaking of his ears, the violins

imitate the braying of an ass, thus foretelling the meta-
morphosis which Apollo meditates inflicting upon him.

In ancient times, music, as is well known, was mainly
religious. Such indeed is the history of all arts, though
gradually they become of a more secular character.
The Hindus believed that a skilful musician was god-
possessed ; probably they still believe this. Krishna,
whose story bears so strange a resemblance to that of
Christ, did not disdain to excel in the playing of the flute.

If we would learn how cathedral music has evolved
from Greek and Roman music, we shall find the history
of this curious transition in Gevaert's learned work on
the subject. This is a book which cannot be recommended indiscriminately ; the fair admirers of our
fashionable novelists would do well to leave it unread.
Saints and Popes have collaborated in this creation of
sacred song. Saint Isidore deals with the diversity of
voices, and, after a lengthy classification, gives the prize
to those that are " high and sweet and clear." To
such, in his opinion, liturgical singing should be restricted.
The deep basses of our parish choirs do not correspond
to such an ideal ; consequently, it is very probable that
plain-chant was originally very different from what it is
nowadays : though we still sing it, in all likelihood
we do not understand it.

" Secondary " music began its first feeble stammer-
ings in Europe during the Middle Ages. In the ninth
century, Guido d'Arezzo set up, in place of the seven
modes of the plain-chant, the modern scale ; the ut (do),
re, mi, fa, etc., being taken from the initial syllables
of the lines of an ancient hymn to Saint John the Baptist ;
this major scale was the beginning of harmony and of

our entire modern musical art. This invention of
genius, it appears, brought the learned eleventh century
monk not only glory but the envy and persecution
with which it is but too frequently accompanied.

The early attempts of "secondary" . . . our own
. . . music to express itself were very strange ; there
was much searching and groping of the way ; the ear
was often diverted from the right track to an extent
that cannot easily be imagined. It was only by degrees
that experience painfully worked out laws which, after
being strictly observed for some time, have progres-
sively widened out and extended their scope until the
domain of music now covers an immense field of activity.
In these modern times of ours, however, this expansion
is no longer sufficient ; these very laws are being repudi-
ated and looked upon as never having been in force
at all, as *non avenues* . . .

CAMILLE SAINT-SAËNS.

OUTSPOKEN ESSAYS ON MUSIC

PART I

THE IDEAS OF M. VINCENT D'INDY

By reason of his talent and erudition, by virtue of his position as the founder of a school, M. Vincent D'Indy has acquired great authority. Everything he writes must of necessity possess considerable influence.

Under the sway of such considerations, it has occurred to me that it might be useful to point out —even though it be to my detriment—certain of his ideas in the " Course of Musical Composition" which do not agree with my own. Not that I claim to be a more or less infallible oracle ; it does not follow, because M. D'Indy's ideas are not always mine, that they are therefore erroneous I will state my arguments : the reader shall judge for himself.

On opening M. D'Indy's book one is immediately

struck with admiration at the loftiness of his conceptions. We see how careful the author is—an attitude which cannot be too greatly admired—to look upon art as one of the most serious things in life. He ascends higher and ever higher until we suffer from vertigo as we follow him, and find that he places art on a level with religious faith, demanding from the artist the three theological virtues—faith, hope, and charity—and not only faith in art, but faith in God! We may remark that Perugini and Berlioz, who were lacking in this faith, were none the less admirable artists, even in the religious style, but we need, not labour the point.

Religions, in themselves admirable objects of art, are incomparable springs of artistic expression. Deduct from architecture, sculpture, painting, even from music itself, everything that deals with religion, and see what is left !

All those Jupiters and Junos, Minervas, Venuses and Dianas, Apollos and Mercuries, Satyrs and Nymphs, those mythological scenes painted on the walls of Pompeii—all that art, which we regard as profane, is religious art. It is the same in Egypt and India, in China and Japan, and even among savage tribes.

Such considerations make it easy to imagine that

art has its source in religion. All the same, its origin is an even more modest one. Art came into being on the day that man, instead of being solely concerned with the utility of an object he had made, concerned himself with its form, and made up his mind that this form should satisfy a need peculiar to human nature, a mysterious need to which the name of " æsthetic sense " has been given.

Afterwards form was enriched by ornament, or decoration, which serves no other purpose than to satisfy this æsthetic sense. Subsequently it became man's desire to reproduce the form of his fellow beings, human and animal, and he began to do this —as a child still does—by a stroke or line. This line does not exist in nature.

Here is the starting point in the radical difference between nature and art ; art is destined not to reproduce nature literally, but to suggest an idea of nature. This principle, badly interpreted, gives rise to the aberrations which manifest themselves at the Salon d'Automne and the Salon des Indépendants.

It is by virtue of this principle that the most insignificant sketch gives an impression of art which will never be supplied by the finest photograph, however " artistic."

It is also on this account that the purists are

mistaken when they attack "imitative music."
Real imitative music would consist of the green-
room noises by which a life-like imitation is given
in the theatre to the wind and the rain and the
various other sounds of nature.   So-called imitative
music does not imitate, it suggests.   Composers
have described storms, but there is not one that is
like any of the rest.   The singing of birds, which
offends certain persons in Beethoven's Pastoral
Symphony, is there imitated in very imperfect
fashion ; it is this very fact that constitutes its
charm.

Nevertheless, it is from the sounds of nature, the
sounds produced by the wind blowing through the
reeds, and more particularly from the utterance of
the human voice, that music had its birth.

When art was born, religion took possession of it.
Religion did not create art.

M. D'Indy, like Tolstoi and M. Barrès and many
other thinkers, seems to see nothing in art but
expression and passion.   I cannot share this
opinion.   To me art is form above all else.

It is perfectly clear that art in general, especially
music, lends itself wonderfully well to expression,
and that is all the amateur expects.   It is quite
different with the artist, however.   The artist who
does not feel thoroughly satisfied with elegant

lines, harmonious colours, or a fine series of chords, does not understand art.

When beautiful forms accompany powerful expression, we are filled with admiration, and rightly so. In such a case, what is it that happens ? Our cravings after art and emotion are alike satisfied. All the same, we cannot therefore say that we have reached the summit of art, for art is capable of existing apart from the slightest trace of emotion or of passion.

This is proved—speaking only of music—by the fact that during the whole of the 16th century there were produced admirable works entirely devoid of emotion.* Their true purpose is thwarted when an attempt is made to render them expressive. Wherein does the Kyrie of the famous Missa Papæ Marcelli express supplication ? Here there is absolutely nothing else than form. On the other hand, see to what a low level music descends when it disdains form and sets emotion in the forefront !

It may here be worth while informing amateurs that music is not—as Victor Hugo has well said in giving form to the most widespread of all feelings— the *vapeur de l'art ;* it is a plastic art, one that is made up of forms. True, these forms exist only in

---

* There are a few exceptions, notably in Palestrina's ' Stabat Mater.'

B

the imagination, and yet, does art as a whole exist in any other way ? These forms are but imperfectly reproduced in musical writing, though sufficiently to suggest it. On this account music should not be written with figures which represent nothing to the eye. It is also for this reason that those who do not read music have some difficulty in forming an idea of it, unless they happen to be gifted with a special aptitude for this art. To them it is indeed the *vapeur de l'art*, a source of sensations and nothing else, and so we find that they take pleasure in listening to the most divergent works, the finest and the most despicable alike ; they see no difference in them.

In the introduction of his book, M. D'Indy says the most excellent things about artistic conscious-ness, the necessity of acquiring talent as the result of hard work and of not relying solely on one's natural endowments. Horace had said the same thing long ago ; still, it cannot be repeated too often at a time like the present, when so many artists reject all rules and restrictions, declare that they mean " to be laws unto themselves," and reply to the most justifiable criticisms by the one per-emptory argument that they " will do as they please." Assuredly, art is the home of freedom, but freedom is not anarchy, and it is anarchy that

is now fashionable both in literature and in the arts.
Why do poets not see that, in throwing down the
barriers, they merely give free access to mediocri-
ties, and that their vaunted progress is but a rever-
sion to primitive barbarism ?

It is no longer necessary to know how to draw or
to paint ; things absolutely devoid of form—I dare
not call them works—find admirers everywhere.
Architecture attempted to follow this trend, but as
houses *must* stand upright, and as they *must* be
habitable, it had to call a halt along this particular
path of folly. The other arts, finding nothing to
hinder them, plunged forward in thoughtless
delirium.

Fétis had foreseen the coming of the " omnitonic "
system. " Beyond that," he said, " I see nothing
further." He could not predict the birth of cacophony, of pure *charivari*.

Berlioz speaks somewhere of atrocious modulations which introduce a new key in one section of
the orchestra while another section is playing in the
old one. At the present time as many as three
different tonalities can be heard simultaneously.

Everything is relative, we are told. That is true,
though only within certain limits which cannot be
overstepped. After a severe frost, a temperature of
twelve degrees above zero seems stiflingly hot ; on

returning from the tropics, you shiver with cold at eighteen degrees above zero. There comes a limit, however, beyond which both cold and heat disorganise the tissues and render life impossible.

The dissonance of yesterday, we are also told, will be the consonance of to-morrow ; one can grow accustomed to anything. Still, there are such things in life as bad habits, and those who get accustomed to crime, come to an evil end. . . .

It is impossible for me to regard scorn of all rules as being equivalent to progress, by which word we generally mean improvement. The true meaning of the word—*progressus*—is a going forward, but the end or object is not stated. There is such a thing as the progress of a disease, and this is anything but improvement.

The more civilization advances, the more the artistic sense seems to decline : a grave symptom. We have already said that art came into existence on the day when man, instead of being solely preoccupied with the utility of an object, began to concern himself with its form.

More and more at the present time does attention to utility assume the foremost place ; we do away with all adornment and trouble ourselves nothing about form. The need to know is being substituted for the need to believe and to admire ; and since

what we know is insignificant compared with what
we do not know, there is an immense field open to
the human intellect.   Nothing will ever again check
the march of science, though this latter is deadly to
faith and art.   Faith defends itself with all its
might, and it is able to make a prolonged defence ;
but what can art do ?   It languishes and dies
wherever our civilization spreads its tentacles.   No
longer is it a necessity for us ; it is a luxury that
appeals only to the *élite*.   Even the beauties of
nature are attacked ; animal species are massacred
and disappear for ever ; age-long forests are
destroyed, never to be restored.   The same thing
happens to cataracts and waterfalls ; nowadays we
think of them as merely so much motor-power.

In dividing music into its three essential parts,
rhythm, melody and harmony, M. D'Indy very
judiciously accords the first place to rhythm.   Let
us therefore see what interpretation he puts on it.

What sets me at ease in discussing the ideas of
M. D'Indy is the fact that, as he himself confesses,
these ideas are very frequently not his own at all, but
rather those of Hugo Riemann, a German.

Here we have an instance of the practice so often
indulged in before the war—and not in music alone
—of crossing the Rhine in our search after truth.
Thus also Combarieu endeavoured to instil into our

minds the wild and senseless ideas of Westphal, who
wished to apply the principles of Greek scansion to
the execution of the works of Bach, Beethoven, &c.,
which are in no way connected therewith. M.
D'Indy gives us elaborate notes on Riemann, Haupt-
mann, Helmholtz, von Ottingen. . . .

When we hear successive sounds of equal duration
like those of the metronome, one of the two has
more intensity than the other ; we can at will, M.
D'Indy tells us, attribute to the more intense sound
the odd numbers :

1, 2, *3*, 4, *5*, 6, *7*, 8.

or the even numbers :

1, *2*, 3, *4*, 5, *6*, 7, *8*.

" The possibility we have of choosing by a mere
effort of will one or the other of these inequalities,
clearly proves that rhythm proceeds not from the
sounds themselves *but from a necessity of our own
mind.* . . . "

This is not the case ; we are not able to choose.
We may do so by a momentary effort, but that is
unnatural ; and if the rhythm is prolonged, nature
resumes her rights and the more intense sound is
seen to belong to the odd numbers.

Robert Schumann, whose reason was not very
clear—it is well-known that he died insane—took

into consideration only his own will when he
neglected the requirements of nature ; along these
lines he committed the greatest of errors.

One of his most characteristic aberrations is in the
Scherzo of his famous Quintet :

Anyone not acquainted with this piece by actually
reading the notes, but only by ear, hears it as
follows :

The idea, as conceived by the author, is original
and vivid ; the result, to the uninformed listener,
is a platitude.   But what does that matter ?   It is
Schumann, and so admiration is forthcoming all the
same.

According to M. D'Indy, measure would appear
to be the enemy of rhythm, " and it is not unreason-

able to think that, untrammelled in the future as it was in the past, *rhythm* will again hold sovereign sway over music, and free it from the servitude in which it has been kept, for nearly three centuries, by the usurping and depressing domination of misunderstood *measure*."

Hitherto, however, it had seemed as though the invention of measure had been a step in advance. I appeal for confirmation of this view to all who have undertaken the task of deciphering old manuscripts of music, from which the measure bar was absent. Did it not create syncopation ? Has it ever prevented the emphasis or accent from falling where it pleased ? M. D'Indy claims that the first beat of the bar is more frequently than not a rhythmically feeble beat. I have not noticed this, but rather the contrary, I imagine. It would, however, prove that measure does not follow rhythm. Shall we have to return to the time when measure was not indicated ? Certain bold innovators have attempted this, though without success. In the music of the Middle Ages, of which M. D'Indy gives instances and which are referred to under the name of plain-song, created before the barbaric invention of measure, I look in vain for rhythm ; it is only absence of rhythm that I find.

Perhaps it is the same with rhythm as with so

many things about which it is impossible to come to
an understanding, because different meanings are
given to the same word. . . .

Let us pass on to melody

In all melody, M. D'Indy (or is it Riemann ?)
assures us, there is a *preparation*, designated, I know
not why, by the Greek word *anacrusis*.

Ah ! qu'en termes galants ces choses-là sont dites !

How often have I made an anacrusis without
knowing it, as M. Jourdain made prose !

In the *Adagio* of Beethoven's fifth Symphony,
where we have the theme :

the first two notes are, I suppose, an anacrusis.
The amazing thing is that sometimes, when there
is no anacrusis, it is taken for granted as existing.

Sufficient for the anacrusis when the phrase
begins on a light beat.   But what are we to say of
the following way of presenting the famous phrase
of the Ninth Symphony ? :

The first bar, then, is nothing more than a

preparation, and the melody really begins only at the second bar !

Do not the first and the third bars belong to the tonic, the second and the fourth to the dominant ? When the tonic and the dominant are both present, is it not to the former that importance is attached ? My entire musical sense rebels against the contrary interpretation, which seems to me a grave error of style.

It is far worse in the first phrase of the Pastoral Symphony, which M. D'Indy presents thus :

and he remarks that this passage is generally " interpreted with the most erroneous accentuation it is possible to give it, as follows :

a deplorable result of the tyranny of the measure-bar and of the antirhythmical teaching of the *solfeggio*."

Now, this is how Beethoven wrote the theme :

The two detached notes, B flat and D, an indication which M. D'Indy has changed into a tie that
extends right to the following C, naturally carry the
accent on to this C. Consequently this interpretation is not the " most erroneous possible " ; it is
the very one intended by the composer. Beethoven could not foresee the theories of M. Riemann
and arrange his music in accordance with his
principles. Is that a matter for regret ?

I will not follow the author in his learned dissertations on plain-song, not considering myself competent in this direction, although I had a great
deal to do with plain-song during my long career
as an organist. I will simply mention the comparison that is made—an original though very
specious one—of the *vocalises* of plain-song with
those fine ornamental capitals seen in missals,
and the same *vocalises* characterized by demisemi-
quavers which conclude an organ piece by Sebastian
Bach.

In the passage cited from this latter, I note an
error that surprises me in so conscientious a writer
as M. D'Indy : a *poco ritenuto* which the composer
had not indicated. Throughout the entire " Course
of Musical Composition " we find these superfluous
indications, unnecessary ties, and added nuances.
The system of the perpetual *legato* did not exist at

the time of Bach ; the clavecin was incapable of expressing nuances, as also was the organ previous to the modern swell. This was not the case with other instruments or with the human voice, but the probable reason why nuances were not indicated is that they were not of the same importance as they are at the present time, when the nuance frequently forms an integral part of the idea ; they were left to the whim of the performer. Why therefore impose arbitrary nuances on the artless reader, who naturally attributes them to the composer ? This system, far too prevalent, whilst deserving of criticism in a serious edition, has nothing to do with a " Course of Composition." One may well wonder why M. D'Indy, instead of taking his quotations from the Peters Edition, which is concerned but slightly with the question of authenticity, did not have recourse to the magnificent edition of the Bachgesellschaft, which does not contain a single detail that is not true to the composer's manuscripts.

* * * * *

In these modern days harmony is the flesh and blood of music, rhythm is the ossature on which it is built up, and melody is its epidermis.

Harmony, we are told, is the daughter of melody. This is a widespread opinion, though it is not my own.

Harmony was developed subsequent to melody, seeing that an advanced musical culture is necessary for appreciating the interest and charm of simultaneous sounds ; harmony, however, previously existed in the sonorous body which makes its harmonics heard, forming an accord with the fundamental sound. More particularly is this phenomenon perceptible in bells, which often give forth a chord that consists entirely of harmonic sounds, the fundamental sound being scarcely perceptible.

One night, in the absolute silence of the country, I heard an immense chord of extreme tenuity ; this chord increased in intensity and resolved itself into a single note produced by the flight of a mosquito.

Subsequently, in Cochin-China, I heard a powerful chord produced by the flight of an enormous coleopter, resounding in the vast sonorous rooms open to every wind—one of those insects that are so common in that wonderful clime. What an enchanted fairy-land are those tropical regions ! And yet I found there a poet insensible to this beauty ; he sent me some of his effusions in which he regretted the fact that he was not in some northern clime, listening to Wagner's operas. " We should never understand each other," I replied, " better not see one another at all ! " And in

my indignation—*facit indignatio versus*—I wrote
the piece in which I hurled insults at Wotan, the
Valkyries, *le Nord, l'horrible Nord!* It was the
Pole I ought to have said, for the extreme South
is in no way behind its *confrère;* only it has no
gods and poets of its own—no one ever thought
of them. In default of gods and poets, however,
it now has its martyrs. . . . .

No ; melody does not produce harmony. If
such were the case, Gregorian chants, folk-songs,
composed without accompaniment of any kind,
would gain by being accompanied. The contrary
is the case ; accompanied, they lose their entire
character and charm.

On the other hand, harmony may produce
melody. This is what happens in the ballad
" Ange si pur," of " La Favorita." It is nothing
but a succession of chords, the upper register of
which is wedded to the voice. The vocal part
possesses no attraction whatsoever for any one
unacquainted with these chords : it is in the harmony that the idea dwells.

The same thing is found in many passages from
Wagner. The chromatic theme of Tristan :

is devoid of meaning without the chords that accompany it :

Here too the idea is in the harmony. This is why those who seek melody and nothing else in Wagner's operas are quite incapable of understanding his music.

Harmony is based on accord worked out by harmonics ; it is a product of nature, antecedent to the human race. Melody is a creation of man himself.

With this exception, the chapter devoted to harmony and the following chapters to the end of the first book of the " Course of Musical Composition " are full of excellent things. Practically my only regret is the superfluous indications and nuances added on to ancient madrigals, indications perhaps necessary for the actual execution of the pieces, but very undesirable in a treatise which should sacrifice everything to purity of text. However, it is impossible to recommend too earnestly a careful reading of these chapters, for they contain much that is of the utmost utility and benefit.   *   *   *   *   *

In the first book of the " Course " we deal only with the elements of music ; the second introduces us to the very heart of the subject—to musical composition in the strict meaning of the term. A masterly exposition shows us its genesis and also the split that took place in music ; a symphonic current on the one hand, a dramatic current on the other.

The second book is devoted to every form of symphonic music ; a third, still in preparation, will deal with the subject of dramatic music

M. D'Indy is perfectly right in telling us that the study of harmony, counterpoint, and fugue, however useful, is only preparatory, and that, when this is done, the work of construction has still to be learnt, a result obtained only as the outcome of prolonged application. He is right in advocating respect for tradition, without which art is like a tree that has no roots, and he does well in blaming the search after originality at all costs, just as in the first book he deprecated the inconsiderate use of modulation, its aimless and profitless waste of effort. In this connection he quotes some admirable sentences from Ruskin.

" It is to symphonic forms," M. D'Indy tells us, " that we attribute first place, both in power and in importance—the place of honour, which from more or less avowable motives they were so long refused, both in musical schools and in the opinion of the public."

" More or less avowable ! " M. D'Indy can strike hard when he chooses.

The immortal trio—Haydn, Mozart, Beethoven —carried instrumental art to so high a level that it has resulted in illusion.   Is it necessary to remind ourselves that in more ancient times instrumental music was used only in two ways : for dance airs and for voice accompaniment ? The dance air produced the suite.   The suite gave birth to the symphony,* where it has left traces of itself in the form of the minuet.   The latter, by gradually accelerating its movement, has produced the scherzo.

The masterpieces of the three great classics have made us forget too readily that the human voice is the finest of all instruments.   It is the one inimitable instrument, living, divine, even miraculous; for no one can understand how the two ligaments called the vocal cords, and the resonator called the larynx, are capable of producing it.   Those who of recent times have been affecting the most profound scorn for ornamental singing, trills, *vocalises*—though

---

* This word includes the orchestral symphony, the quartet, the sonata, &c.

C

they were utilised by all the great composers of the
past—ought rather to express wonder and amazement thereat.   Berlioz ridiculed singers who succeed in playing on the larynx as one would play
on a flute.   What harm is there in that ?   Neither
Handel, nor Sebastian Bach, nor Mozart, nor
Beethoven, nor Weber, objected to florid singing.
A curious thing to note is that Berlioz, in his lyrical
comedies, also introduced *vocalises*, though he
treats them in a singularly unskilful manner.

Vocalises are absent from the works of
Richard Wagner, though he did employ the trill,
or shake ;   and while the trills of Brünnehilde
are very effective in the " Valkyrie," those in the
duet with Siegfried, on her awakening, seem very
strange to any in the audience who have not been
sufficiently hypnotised by Wagnerian infatuation.

There is no need to conceal from ourselves the
fact that, with the exception of a few special and
comparatively restricted circles, the public prefer
vocal to instrumental music.   The cause of this
is not to be found in more or less avowable reasons ;
it is nature herself that insists upon it, because
the voice is the only natural instrument.   It is
even the one eternal instrument, so far as human
things can be eternal.   Instruments pass and
have their day ;   the instrumental music of the

16th century is for the most part impossible of execution nowadays. But the human voice remains.

In the course of his work, M. D'Indy reverts to this idea ; he insinuates that the love of gain may have something to do with the preference for theatrical form shown by certain composers. As the public has always evinced a marked predilection for this form, no wonder musicians instinctively turn to the kind of music that will enable them to earn their living ; not every one has the good fortune to be born with a silver spoon in his mouth. All the same, there must be some other reason, for almost all composers have written for the theatre or have tried to do so. M. D'Indy himself has been attracted in this direction.

Love of gain was not the incentive which made Richard Wagner embark upon his colossal work, the " Ring of the Nibelung," under conditions of so exceptional a nature that he did not know if it would ever be produced.

Meyerbeer was possessed of a great fortune, the major portion of which was swallowed up in his musical works. In his memoirs, Duprez artlessly tells how the gifted composer made every possible sacrifice to ensure the execution of his operas, and how the famous singer profited thereby.

Haydn wrote Italian operas in his youth. During his stay in London, when producing his finest symphonies for the Salomon concerts, he began an " Orfeo " which he never finished, owing to the fact that the theatre at which it was to have been given went bankrupt.

Mozart would still be Mozart, even if there remained nothing but his theatrical works.

The reason why Beethoven confined himself to the symphony and did not devote himself to the theatre is that the Opera of Vienna would not have it so. Beethoven had actually offered to undertake the production of one work each year for five years.

No one can tell what would have happened if Beethoven's offer had not been refused, if he had acquired that theatrical experience which cannot be had apart from the theatre and which is evident in the second version of " Fidelio " when compared with the first " Leonora." Certain parts of " Fidelio " are not inferior to any of his works : the famous " Pistol " scene resembles nothing that had hitherto been given. Had Beethoven been able to realise his desires, the very direction in which the lyrical theatre was tending would probably have been quite different.

Both Mendelssohn and Schumann tried the theatre. The failure of Schumann's " Genevieve " —interesting as it was from a musical point of view, though anything but adapted for the theatre, —was what determined his hostility to Meyerbeer ; he could not understand how such music could be regarded as *music*, though he must have realised that the theatre has to accept art forms inadmissible elsewhere. The painting of stage scenery is different from painting on an easel. Wagner placed the purely musical, even symphonic, interest in the foreground ; but success was achieved only as the result of pressure directed upon the public, the duration and intensity of which were such that nothing like it up to that time had been seen, or probably ever will be again.

Berlioz, after writing the following terrible sentence : " Theatres are the disorderly houses of music, and the chaste Muse one drags therein cannot enter without shuddering," treated thus his own Muse, and certainly the result was not always satisfactory. Nevertheless " Les Troyens " is a superior work, though it was not smiled on by Fortune—that implacable queen who rules over battles and operas alike. Was not preference over it shown to a translation of Bellini's feeble " Romeo," with its loud fanfare of brasses, big drums and cymbals for the occasion ! A blush of shame rises to the cheek at the very thought. However, a notable failure rewarded this ill turn on the part of the then Imperial Academy of Music.

Richard Strauss, after becoming known to the public by symphonic poems, has revolutionised the musical world by extraordinary operas upon which I will not dwell, and thereby avoid irritating his admirers—for he has admirers. Did not one of them state that the fact of writing the song in one key and the accompaniment in another, was a matter of no importance whatsoever.?

Before continuing, I must deal thoroughly with a side question which will necessitate special consideration and may carry me somewhat beyond the limits of this study. I am thinking of an evil that has long affected music, that first made itself felt in pianoforte music and is now threatening to extend its ravages, an evil from whose contagion M. D'Indy himself has not escaped.

*   *   *   *   *

There is not the faintest indication of nuance or of variation of pace in the music of the ancient clavecinists. Probably the movements were less contrasted than they are nowadays, and the *tempo* might have been left to the whim of the executant, except in those extreme cases in which it was indicated. Nuances were not practicable on the clavecin, where *forte* and *piano* were alone possible, because of the different registers with which large instruments were provided. It was Czerny, I imagine, who, when publishing for the pianoforte the clavecin works of Sebastian Bach, enriched them with numerous indications of movements and nuances, of tied and detached notes. The work was carried through in the most arbitrary fashion. Only at a considerably later date, when the numerous cantatas of Bach were rescued from oblivion, was it possible, on comparing them with clavecin pieces, to discover by similitude of form what feelings these latter were capable of expressing. It was then ascertained that Czerny had frequently erred, but he had created a school of music, and his influence had long been felt ; perhaps it continues even up to the present time.

With the appearance of the pianoforte, which allowed of nuances, music has become more coloured. Composers have largely increased the number of their indications or signs. Moreover, as the divergence has become wider between slow movements and lively movements, indications of pace have become necessary. Those of tied and detached notes have also become more frequent.

Judging by the method of playing adopted by

certain elderly persons whom I heard when I was young, I am inclined to believe that, at one period, abuse was made of the detached note, and that this abuse found its reaction in the system of the perpetual *legato*. This system, probably introduced by Kalkbrenner, had met with ill-omened success in France. According to Kalkbrenner, everything was to be tied ; this was a principle, it was not even necessary to indicate it.   In his pianoforte arrangements of Beethoven's Symphonies he writes the theme of the Pastoral Symphony as follows :

depriving it of its articulation, and at the same time of its distinctive character.

The most celebrated professors of the pianoforte, carried away by the force of example, have adopted this method, and have published editions of all the classics which have been subjected to this deplorable system.   Quite recently a new edition of the " Clavecin bien tempéré " presents the theme of the Fugue in D major in the First Book as follows:

thus diminishing the strong and rhythmic character

of the last two beats in the bar.   And yet it is easy
to point out the error in such a system.

When Mozart, in one of his Concertos, after
writing the following passage for the flute :

which shows that the second group of notes alone
must be tied, reproduces the passage in the pianoforte part *with the same indication*, it is quite
evident that his intention is being violated if a
large tie is extended over the whole bar.

When Beethoven, in a Sonata for pianoforte and
violin, gives the violin this figured passage :

the very writing of the passage shows that where
there is no tie a different stroke of the bow is needed
for each note, and when the same passage appears
in the pianoforte part *with the same indication*,
this is certainly done in order that the latter may
reproduce, as far as possible, the effect of the
violin.

When Beethoven, in the Sonata for Pianoforte,
Op. 79, writes :

with the indication *leggieramente,* and then puts
ties over the following passage, it is clear that this
denotes a different execution in the two passages,
and that the former must be understood to be
non legato. The author's thought and intention
are consequently distorted or misrepresented when
ties are scattered about promiscuously.

This *non legato* is not the same as a detached
note. It is produced by a clearness of articulation
and a lightness of touch which enable one to " put
air between the notes," as Liszt said.

When the firm of Breitkopf conceived the idea of
publishing a complete collection of Mozart's works,
in their desire to make it as perfect as possible they
issued an appeal to all who might possess manuscripts of the great composer's, with the object
of producing a *ne varietur* edition. Unfortunately
they entrusted the revision of the Pianoforte
Concertos to Reinecke, who, instead of aiming at
purity of text alone, thought of nothing but
treating these wonderful Concertos in the fashion
of the day. Consequently we find everywhere
such indications as *legato, molto legato, sempre
legato,* frequently running counter to the purpose

of the author himself. He did even worse than this ; but to enter upon such a subject would carry us beyond our present limits.

Germany, alas, was destined to go even farther in distorting his masterpieces !

One day, Westphal came along with his strange invention for applying to the execution of modern music the principles of Greek scansion. This idea, for some reason I do not understand, has had a great vogue, and at the same time done a vast amount of mischief.

An already ancient edition of the celebrated Fugue for clavecin in E minor, by Handel, the theme of which is :

appears as follows :

When the fugue develops and becomes complicated, this accentuation makes it impossible of execution.

Is it not evident that the genesis of the second bar is nothing else than the breaking up of the figure :

and that consequently the last three notes of the third and fourth beats belong to the group of four notes of which they form part, and not to the following group ?

If, therefore, ties were to be introduced—though quite unnecessarily—they ought to have been given thus :

and not in the manner stated.

In the Peters edition a passage from Chopin (First Concerto, *Finale*) which the author has indicated thus :

is disfigured in this way :

and so robbed of all its elegance.

If, however, we would see to what degree of
folly the Westphalian system is capable of leading
us, we must consult the " Analyse thématique,
rythmique, et métrique des Symphonies de Beethoven," made by a Belgian and published at
Brussels, with a eulogistic preface by Combarieu.
At almost every note we find Beethoven put to
school and improved upon !

What he writes thus :

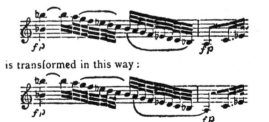

is transformed in this way :

and everything else is dealt with in the same
fashion.

How comes it that M. D'Indy, attentive as he

is to the slightest details, did not more successfully resist the contagion of bad example ?

He protests quite rightly against the superfluous indications, notably the *rallentando* inflicted on the old masters in modern editions ; and yet he himself, in the first part of his book, cites a fragment of Sebastian Bach containing a *rallentando* which the author has not indicated.   A strange contradiction !

In the musical quotations from this second book of the " Course " we find hypothetical indications, arbitrary ties in which the influence of the Westphalian ideas too frequently makes itself felt. Here are a few instances :

The ties weaken the rhythm.

No explanation is given of these two notes tied on to the three, making the playing of the passage inconvenient.

Here are two nuances impossible on the clavecin, as well as ties that are arbitrary.

In the original text the chord in the second bar is noted thus :

Nor is there any reason whatever for tying it on to the preceding bar.

The tie between A and C changes the character of the passage.

In the author's text there is no tie at all, and this one, culminating in an octave in a passage of considerable power, makes it impossible of execution.

Later on, the author, reproducing the same idea in the melody, writes it as follows :

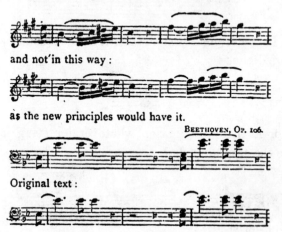

and not'in this way :

as the new principles would have it.

BEETHOVEN, OP. 106.

Original text :

The Westphalian aberrations—of which the examples taken from a Fugue of Handel and a Symphony of Beethoven give a sufficiently clear idea —spring from one initial error, which consists in regarding musical figures in themselves, without taking into account the harmony, expressed or understood, which gives them their meaning. Down to the time of Westphal, all the masters had instinctively been aware of this ; it had guided them in their indications.   All the notes that form part of one and the same chord should, *on principle,* form part of the same group. This is a general rule to which there are many exceptions. Just as the musician has the privilege of writing *syncopations,* he has also that of infringing the above-mentioned rule. A charming example of this may be found in the *Gradus ad Parnassum* of Clementi :

We have no right, however, to turn the exception into the rule, and inflict it on composers against their will.

Now that this long digression is ended, we may return to the study of the " Course of Musical Composition."

*   *   *   *   *

One day, I was utterly stupefied to hear Gevaert, the famous director of the Conservatoire of Brussels, declare that the study of the fugue was unnecessary.

Strange ideas would at times come into his head ; he regarded the Treaty of Berlin as an admirable piece of work ; in architecture, he recognised nothing but the Greek style : all else, according to him, was non-existent. His edition of song classics is unqualifiable. . . .

M. D'Indy is not of Gevaert's opinion as regards

the fugue. He devotes to it a long chapter, admirably documented and detailed, dealing with its origin, its formation, its elements, particularly the canon style, which he considers separately. Amongst all the masters of the past whom he quotes in this connection—Italians, Spaniards, English-men, Germans, and Frenchmen—he naturally gives the place of honour to Sebastian Bach, the Jupiter of the fugue. Amongst the Italians, I looked in vain for the names of Clementi and Cherubini. And yet Clementi has interspersed his immortal " Gradus " with numerous fugues and canons ; and though the fugues may not claim to rival those of the " Clavecin bien tempéré," they are nevertheless very interesting ; the canons are of rare merit and some are real masterpieces. Cherubini wrote a treatise on " Fugue," containing fugues with two, three, and four parts, and finally, a grand fugue with eight parts and two choruses, an admirable piece of work.

When M. D'Indy sets forth the various artifices in the fugue, we may note the ingenious and amusing comparison he makes between a theme dealt with by *augmentation* and by *diminution*, and the effect produced on an object by the apposition of diver-gent and convergent lenses.

M. D'Indy acknowledges that, in spite of the

great changes that have taken place in musical art, the fugue, which has a great deal of vitality, still exists and has its admirers. The only thing is that it is less frequently used; we are no longer " allured " by it; and in these days I find no one capable of producing—as Handel did with the greatest ease—long fugued choruses; we are " allured " by other branches of the art.

Nevertheless the fugue has not altogether disappeared from modern compositions, and M. D'Indy names authors who have kept it alive. He honours me by including my name amongst them, though he finds fault with my fugues for being somewhat cold and conventional. I cannot well judge what concerns myself; still, I hardly think this criticism can be brought against the first *morceau* of my Symphony in A minor, which affects the fugue form.

I remember that at the first performance of this *morceau* the adoption of the fugue form appeared scandalous to many of the listeners. This assuredly was not the opinion of M. D'Indy, who frequently throughout his " Course " praises my works. I am sincerely and deeply grateful to him for this, as he is not lavish with his favours. And in this connection I cannot too strongly insist on the fact that nothing but my love for music is now prompting

me in this task of criticism, and that the word
" criticism " must here be given its very highest
interpretation. So important and conscientious a
work as this " Course of Musical Composition "
frequently deserves admiration, and sympathy
above everything. It would deserve both to a still
greater degree if the author, instead of trusting to
his own intuition, had not sought illumination from
across the Rhine. Nothing could be better than
to go to Germany for masterpieces, but do not go
there for theories . . . Even Richard Wagner's
theories are often pernicious ; his works would not
be what they are if he had always conformed to his
theories ; the harm they have done is incalculable.
M. Debussy has been highly praised for avoiding
them. True, his music in no way resembles that of
the author of " Tristan " ; but he none the less
applied, as completely as he could, the Wagnerian
system, which consists in diverting interest from
the singing and bestowing it on the orchestra.

Before leaving the fugue I cannot help remarking
that this part of the " Course " appears to me
calculated rather to show the pupil how others have
written fugues than to teach him to write them
himself. In this connection, it is my opinion that
Cherubini's time-honoured treatise might be put to
more profitable use.

*   *   *   *   *

We will not follow M. D'Indy in his learned and circumstantial dissertations on the various forms which music has successively adopted throughout the ages : the suite, a series of dance airs ; the sonata, of which Beethoven is the hero, as he is of the symphony (which is nothing more than a sonata for the orchestra) ; the variation, to which he rightly attaches great importance.   All this is of the utmost interest.

With reference to dance airs, I am not sure that the author has been sufficiently informed as regards the pavane, which he simply mentions—in passing— as an air in duple time.   With many others I have long thought that the pavane was an air of a dainty, elegant character, after the style of the famous Romanesca.   A pavane of this description, by Auguste Durand, has long enjoyed considerable favour, while everyone is acquainted with the delightful pavane of M. Gabriel Fauré.   I myself have introduced dainty pavanes in " Etienne Marcel " and in " Proserpine."

Quite different is the origin of the pavane, which dates back to the 16th century.   When I formed the idea of introducing contemporary music into the ballet of " Ascanio," I went to the Bibliothèque Nationale and undertook a certain amount of research work which culminated in an unexpected discovery : pompous and majestic pavanes in three-and four-time. Most likely they were intended to accompany a solemn march-past, or processions during which a certain amount of " strutting " was indulged in, consisting, as they did, of a few bars repeated indefinitely, until the *Coda* brought the whole to a conclusion. The first *morceau* in the ballet of " Ascanio " is a three-time pavane ; the last a four-time pavane, both of them authentic as regards not only the melody but also the *ensemble*. In the original, the first pavane is written in six real parts, which I have retained.

I am very pleased to find that M. D'Indy attaches great importance to Haydn's sonatas. These are not known to the youth of the present day, who are ignorant of their beauty, their extraordinary fecundity, and that wealth of imagination possessed by the musician to whom we are indebted for Mozart and Beethoven. When we plunge into the score of his great Oratorio, " The Seasons," we imagine we have discovered a new planet. This many-sided work, ranging from comic opera to sacred music, representing as it does the thousand varied aspects of nature, the purity of the entire plan combining with the warmest and richest colouring—this work, so varied in form, ought frequently to be offered to the public, and every composer should study it thoroughly.

I regret to have to point out once more, in Beethoven's " Farewell " sonata, Op. 81*a*, the tendency to substitute arbitrary indications for those given by the author. Where Beethoven wrote :

we find :

a very different thing, both from the point of view of style and from that of execution.

As regards variation and embellishments, M. D'Indy speaks of the Italian *gruppetto* which Richard Wagner so widely encroached upon in his works—to such an extent that it was, quite incorrectly, designated the " groupe wagnérien." He thought of remodelling this ornament in his latest works for the purpose of rejuvenating it. This *gruppetto* is quite worthless and antiquated. It was going out of fashion, and Wagner would have done better not to restore it to a place of honour. I should have been glad to find M. D'Indy sharing this opinion of mine, but to every true Wagnerite Wagner is a god whose most insignificant acts are sacred. His will be done ! Such is the rule, from which there can be no deviation.

On the other hand, I find him very severe in his judgment on Dussek, and on the same composer's sonata, " The Return to Paris," which enjoyed a temporary celebrity. The *Scherzo* (to which, however, M. D'Indy renders justice), with its enharmonic theme, is extraordinarily audacious for the period in which it was written.

Perhaps he does not attach sufficient importance to the medial part in the movement in the ternary section, which begins the second part. In Mozart, it is frequently here that we find the main interest of the movement. For instance, at the beginning of the second part of an entrancing sonata in C we find this amazing and delightful *false relation* :

which nothing in the first part had led us to expect.

It was left to Mozart to discover that there are two kinds of false relation : the one which offends the ear and must be avoided, the other which is a source of beauty, and was extensively used by himself.

M. D'Indy has a high opinion of the sonatas of T. W. Rust, upon which he dwells at length, regarding them as superior to those of Haydn and of Mozart. It would be wise to proceed warily as regards Rust's compositions, concerning the authenticity of which there has been much dispute.

These sonatas have been considerably altered. Probably M. D'Indy was not aware that musical "faking" is a common practice in Germany. Amateur works which have reached the publisher and unfortunately bear traces of their origin, subsequently appear embellished with all the graces of the most refined composition. Was there not even published a posthumous Violin Concerto by Beethoven, of which the author had written no more than a few bars ?

Rust's grandson has protested against the authenticity of the famous sonatas, but to no purpose ; M. D'Indy had caught his great composer and was unwilling to let him go.

*   *   *   *   *

We may wonder at the inordinate height of the pedestal upon which he has erected the statue of César Franck, the " gifted continuer of the great German symphonist, the greatest creator of musical forms along with Beethoven and Wagner." It would be ungracious for me to dispute the merit of his works, as I was one of the first to give them a hearing, and at my own risk, at a time when the public still disregarded them. Further, Jules Simon, then Minister of Education, had consulted me on the choice of a professor for the organ at the Conservatoire, and I strongly recommended him to choose César Franck, so that the latter, with the help of the salary granted by the State, might not find himself compelled to waste in giving pianoforte lessons the time he could more profitably devote to composition. All the same, though I highly esteem his works and endeavour to get them appreciated at their true value, I have never gone so far as to set them on a level with those of the great masters of music ; they lack too many qualities for that distinction Berlioz was more of an artist than a musician ; Franck was more of a musician than an artist : he was not a poet.   In his works we do not find that latent warmth, that irresistible charm which makes us forget everything and transports us into unknown and supernal realms.   The sense of the picturesque seems absent from them.   At one moment we come up against an ill-timed modulation—as in his Sonata for pianoforte and violin—where we are forcibly transported from E major to B flat minor, the latter key thus acquiring, as it were, an unpleasant bitterness* ; at another moment we have a construction in which something is lacking, as in the " Prélude, Choral, et Fugue," " an imperishable work, *monumentum ære perennius*," a *morceau* anything but pleasant or convenient to play, where the choral is not a choral nor the fugue a fugue, for it speedily falls all to pieces, and continues in interminable digressions which no more resemble a fugue than a zoophyte resembles a mammifer. These digressions are scarcely atoned for by a brilliant ending. Assuredly it is not in this way that we shall, even at the present time, understand the possibilities of the time-honoured venerable fugue.

César Franck made use very frequently—even too frequently—of the canon ; but his canons are always either in unison or in octaves, thus presenting no difficulty of any kind. His much-vaunted work, " Les Béatitudes," is very unequal in merit. Occasionally we meet with something quite insignificant ; nor is the declamation invariably free from reproach. Speaking generally, we are more likely to find in him a violent and meritorious aspiration

* The first part of this sonata is delightful—but as for the rest ! Still, it has acquired fame ; consequently there is nothing more to be said. I may, however, confess that I prefer M. Gabriel Fauré's admirable Sonata in A.

towards beauty than true beauty itself. His efforts
remind us of Victor Hugo's act of faith in God :

" Il est, il est, il est, il est éperdument "

His emotion is seldom communicative ; I say
seldom, I do not say *never*. It is a pleasure for me
to cite the beautiful soprano air in " The Redemption," illuminating and cheering this austere landscape as does the sun with his genial beams.

At times a gloomy sadness hangs over his work,
so that when listening to it we are conscious of a
pleasure which may be compared with that afforded
by the Psalms of David at a Church service. But
this is neither the tragic and splendid sadness of
Mozart in his Fantasia in C minor nor that of
Beethoven in his celebrated Sonata in C sharp minor.
His teaching did not always meet with brilliant
results, consisting as it did, for the most part, of
compliments and encouragement which, coming
from so exalted a source, charmed his pupils and
converted them into enthusiastic disciples, prose-
lytes of the Master. One of them, who was very
intelligent, not happening to find in César Franck
the help requisite for completing the instrumentation of a work which he had outlined, called on me
for advice. Three series of painstaking consulta-
tion-lessons enabled him to bring out the only

orchestral composition by which he is known to the public. All the same, he did not advertise the fact, and, in the eyes of the world, he remained César Franck's pupil.

Franck's religious music, though eminently deserving of respect, calls to mind the austerities of the cloister rather than the perfumed splendours of the sanctuary.

There can be no doubt that M. D'Indy is the favourite disciple to whom the master unveiled the holy of holies and exposed the treasures of his doctrine, the result being that a sense of gratitude influences his judgment. The same feeling makes me regret that Liszt does not occupy a more important place in the " Course of Musical Composition." His great fantasia, entitled " Sonate," and the Symphonic Poems are disposed of in a few words and relegated to the Variations. The " Sonate," long neglected, is now likely to become famous, and the same might be said concerning his great Fantasia for the Organ on the Choral of the " Prophête," *Ad nos, ad salutarem undam*, were it easier to find an opportunity of listening to it in France. In England and America, however, where every concert-hall is provided with an organ and where Protestantism permits of sacred concerts being given in places of worship, it takes its rightful place.

The creation of the symphonic poem would be sufficient in itself to immortalise its author. This *genre*, to which the most varied forms may be applied, shows a tendency to take the place of the symphony, strictly so called, which now seems to have reached its full expansion, and, like the sonata, no longer has anything of importance to teach us.

Like Haydn and Mozart, like most too prolific artists, Liszt has written things that are unnecessary ; the purest taste does not always govern his style. The same may be said of many great artists and poets. It is scarcely necessary to do more than mention a few chance names that come to mind : Rubens, Verdi, Shakespeare, Goethe, Victor Hugo. The latter even went so far as to say that lack of taste was a sign of genius.

Liszt's music has long been calumniated and traduced. Whereas certain critics looked upon it as " pianist's music," others accused the author of introducing philosophical systems into music. At last justice is being meted out to him, and I congratulate myself on being one of the first to plead his cause against the general hostility.

In bringing to a conclusion this short critical survey, I wish to express my regret at being unable to carry it further, M. D'Indy's work being still incomplete. With his great erudition and his power of analysis, he has much more that is interesting to tell us, and I earnestly hope that I may see the completion of the "Course of Musical Composition."

It is also my desire, by this brief study, to draw attention to so fine a work and to increase the number of its readers.

THE MANUSCRIPT LIBRETTO OF "FAUST."

WHEN and on what occasion did Gounod make me a present of this manuscript ? I am unable to say definitely, though doubtless it was very shortly after the appearance of his famous work. Interesting by reason of the information it supplies on the genesis of " Faust," it is also valuable on account of the numerous musical annotations written on the margin, thus giving us the first spontaneous thoughts of the composer. I feel that these annotations are deserving of being more widely known.

Before undertaking this work let us glance at the various ways in which French artists have dealt with that episode of Goethe's poem which in the public mind represents him as a whole, just as the episode of Francesca da Rimini sums up the whole of Dante's " Divine Comedy," though it is merely a tiny fragment thereof.

In Goethe's poem the name of the young *amoureuse* is Gretchen—*i.e.*, Margot. She is simply

52

the maid-servant of Dame Martha, in whose garden takes place the conversation between the four *dramatis personæ*. The first time I saw Goethe's " Faust " played in a German theatre I was quite astonished to behold, appearing unexpectedly on the stage during the *kermesse*, a slightly-built brunette who replied to Faust's compliments in scandalised accents : " Je ne suis pas une demoiselle, je ne suis pas belle. . . . ." and then rapidly hid away in the crowd. She was anything but the ideal fair-complexioned creature with whom Ary Scheffer has familiarised us (coming out of church with angelic mien, while Faust looks on enraptured), or the fanciful creation which Gounod's music has popularised.

Previously we had the " Damnation of Faust " by Berlioz, where Marguerite, " while binding her hair," sings the " Chanson du Roi de Thulé," which the author calls a Gothic song, and which begins with that augmented 4th interval abhorred of ancient music, followed by ultra-modern chromatic successions. Distorted and unlovely though it be, this song none the less possesses the special quality of *character* in the highest degree. From what source then did it draw its inspiration ? From the sketches of " Faust " made by Delacroix, a series of ultra-romantic lithographs in which the

E

person of Gretchen is strangely transformed ?
It is said that Goethe, when he saw them, affirmed
that they completely expressed his own thought.
The old, old comedy of great men flattering one
another in order to create admirers ! The sketches
of Delacroix are in the first rank of artistic production, but they do not represent Goethe's
" Faust."

The Marguerite and the Faust of Gounod differ
so strikingly from their models that in Germany
the famous opera is given the name of
" Margarethe."

The Marguerite of Berlioz differs even more from
the German Gretchen than does that of Gounod.
She does not sit at her spinning-wheel, nor is she
accompanied by Dame Martha. Here we have an
ideal creature, appearing in a dream, if not in a
vision, and Faust orders Mephisto to find her for
him. There is nothing of this in Goethe's poem ;
we now have the French Marguerite, whom our
public will accept in no other guise.

When I was a child there took place in Paris a
thing delightful to behold : the military retreat,
an ingenious combination of trumpets and drums
that has long been discontinued. I can still recall
the shades of night beginning to invade the Jar-
din du Luxembourg, the shooting stars—then an

unexplained phenomenon—falling across the sky, and the drums and trumpets making a complete tour of the immense vault of heaven and ravishing my youthful senses as the strains alternately approached and died away in the distance. Berlioz heard and rightly appreciated this retreat ; and, replacing the drums with *timbales*, blending the plaintive wail of the abandoned Marguerite with the distant songs of the students, he made this the background of a twilight scene, quite charming and striking in its originality, while essentially French in character.

We are but too well acquainted with the present form of the retreat : not only is there no balanced combination of drums and trumpets, but the refrain itself, quite different from the old one, is executed " to order," without either rhythm or time, and in the most anti-musical fashion imaginable. And we are said to have made progress in music because the public has become accustomed to being bored and rapturously applauds things it is utterly incapable of understanding !

Berlioz insisted on pointing out how different his " Faust " was from the original. " I have written," he said, " the *Damnation* de Faust." In Goethe's poem Faust is *saved*. Many parts of this opera

are his own creation, notably the famous " Course
à l'abîme." Many others are adapted from the
Weimar poet, including the " Chanson du Rat,"
which he might well have omitted, for the whole
of its value disappears in imitation ; the refrain,
built up on an untranslatable play upon words, here
becomes a platitude :

> Aussi triste, aussi misérable
> Que s'il eut eu l'amour au corps !

But, after all, platitudes are frequent enough in
the text of the " Damnation of Faust," and great
is the contrast between the wealth of the music
and the poverty of the poem. How did it come
about that the literary Berlioz, the fervent admirer
of Victor Hugo, consented to bless this ill-matched
union ? Why did the critics, so strict against
Scribe and other librettists, show such utter
indifference before this anomaly ? The gold and
diamond embroidered mantle flung over this
poverty hides it from view : let us not remove
the veil !

On opening the libretto of " Faust," many
are the surprises that await us. In the first
place we are struck with the changes made in the
work during rehearsal. No doubt some of these
alterations the authors would have made of their
own accord, but in this particular case we see the

influence of the celebrated conductor Carvalho,
a nervous man of perpetually changing humour
and restless imagination. When he took up an
opera, although one that had long been famous and
was of world-wide renown, it must bear the impress
of his individuality. To quote only one instance :
it was he who conceived the strange idea, in the
second Act of " Orphée," of substituting for
Eurydice an " Ombre heureuse " of which no one
had ever dreamt, and which still persists, an
outrage on commonsense, in Gluck's masterpiece.
As may be imagined, it was far worse when a new
drama was brought to him. He had but one thing
in his mind—to add his own ideas on to those of the
author. The place and time of the action were
continually changing ; unexpected episodes arose
in his excited brain ; *morceaux* slowly worked out
in the silence of the study had to disappear and
make room for hurried improvisations. But all
this came to an end when Massenet brought him
the score of " Manon," containing the imprint
Ne varietur. At last he had found his master.

" Faust " was originally written in the opéra-
comique form, with dialogue. A delightful form,
dating back to the most remote times ; one to which
the public has never been hostile, though it would
tend to disappear had it not been retained in the

operetta. " Faust " was performed in this dress until the time when its introduction at the Opera compelled the abandonment of the spoken word. Many musical treats owe their existence to this event, which gave the work the form it definitely assumed.

Jules Barbier and Michel Carré, interested in the subject, heartily gave themselves up to their task. Their first project was far too long ; numerous suppressions or " cuts " proved inevitable. Any who are curious to know what fragments were omitted will find most of them in the handsome *brochure* of Albert Soubies and Henri de Curzon entitled " Documents inédits sur le Faust de Gounod."

In the very first scene, Gounod appreciably abridged the monologue of Faust, where we find a great difference between the French copy and the German original. In the latter, the sound of the Easter bells and the singing of the choir cause the murderous cup to fall from Faust's hands ; in the French libretto, he is arrested in his purpose by the fresh ringing voices of the young peasant girls and the rugged chants of the ploughmen as they praise the charms of nature. In the final apotheosis the religious choruses are suppressed.

After this scene, Wagner and Siebel, the master's

two pupils, come to converse with him, as in the original. There are here the words of a *Terzetto ;* I do not know if it was ever written. In the French score, the purpose of the coming of these characters was to inform the public of Siebel's love for Marguerite, to prepare the way for the appearance of the heroine. The *preparation !* This was at that time a dogma, as were the three unities in bygone times. When the Opéra obstinately refused to produce " Samson et Dalila " I requested an influential person to give me his support. He replied that my work was not playable, because the character of Dalila was not *prepared.*

However it be, Wagner and Siebel disappeared from the first Act, then known as the Prologue. They reappeared only in the following Act, Wagner to recite a few bars of the " Chanson du Rat," fortunately interrupted by Mephistopheles, and Siebel to become the youth, who is chastely in love, as we know, with Marguerite.

It is with Mephistopheles that the musical annotations begin, written in pencil on the margin. The first are of no great interest, and differ but little from the finally accepted text. Here the principle of the *preparation* served the authors well.

In Goethe's poem Mephistopheles causes a number of women to appear before Faust, and when

later on he accosts Gretchen, it is by chance :
the old *savant* who had hitherto lived alone with
his musty old volumes and his retorts, when
transformed into a young man, falls in love with
the first pretty girl he meets.

Here we have the ravishing vision of Marguerite at the spinning-wheel, to the accompaniment of heavenly music, awakening love
in the heart of Faust and deciding him to affix
his signature to the devilish pact.

And now we come to the joyous gaiety and ex-
citement of the *kermesse*. May I be permitted to
state at this point, and in parenthesis, how greatly
I deplore the fact that in Paris, as everywhere
else, this *morceau* is distorted and misrepresented
by too rapid a *tempo*. The deliciously charming
" Chœur des Vieillards " becomes a gross caricature,
and the *ensemble* is nothing but an inharmonious
and displeasing hullabaloo.

Then followed a farewell scene between Valentin
and Marguerite, giving occasion for a long duet
which Gounod set to music. This scene was a mistake, and ought to have been dispensed with ; it disregarded the effect of the appearance of Marguerite
on the occasion of her first meeting with Faust.
But it was a delight to hear Madame Carvalho
in the rôle of Marguerite, with that incomparable

voice and wonderful delivery of hers. The final
ensemble of the duet :

seemed to reverberate in the orchestra when,
previous to the " Air des Bijoux," Marguerite says
pensively " Me voilà toute seule ! "

It must not be imagined that the song of the
" Veau d'Or " was a spontaneous production, like
Minerva springing fully armed from the head of
Jupiter. The Calf, in the first instance, was a
Beetle " which had proved very successful."
As this original song did not please—I do not know
why—the authors tried several others, of which
not a trace remains, before deciding upon the one
with which we are acquainted.

To proceed to the following Act. With the
" Air des Bijoux " we enter upon interesting
musical annotations that began in this way :

Fortunately these octave leaps and unnecessary modulations have disappeared.

Nor has there remained any trace of these changes on resuming the motive :

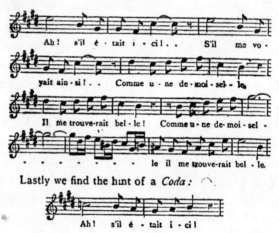

Lastly we find the hint of a *Coda :*

which was left unfinished.

Now we enter into the drama . . . and also into the tragi-comedy of endless changes and modifications introduced not only at the rehearsals but even at the public performances, year after year. As each theatrical season came round and the work was taken up afresh, the indefatigable conductor brought forward new ideas, and the authors, not having the courage to oppose him, adopted his views. There were cuttings here,

and additions there, along with a general upsetting
of the order of the scenes.

Originally the third Act began at a cross-road :
" On the right, the church ; on the left, Marguerite's house.   Near the threshold a stone bench
in front of which stands a spinning-wheel.   In the
centre a fountain."

Young maidens entered singing, carrying pitchers
on their shoulders as they made their way towards
the fountain.   This took up an entire scene, with
choruses carrying on a dialogue and a *coryphée*
named Lise, who was to sing three couplets.
Three were evidently too many, for Gounod
retained only the third, as follows :

Le beau sé - duc - teur . . vê - tu d'or,

La char - ma, dit - on . . dès l'a · bord:

Mais les pleurs sont voi - sins du ri · rè. . .

Car un beau ma - tin, sans rien di · · ·

· · · · re, Le ga - lant é - tran - ger s'en fuit.

The final bars are missing ; it is the termination
of the air resumed by the chorus which alone
has been retained, the cross-road having disappeared to give place to Marguerite's chamber.
We can do no more than form suppositions regarding the harmonies which were to accompany
this dainty couplet.

The maidens having departed, Marguerite sat
down at her spinning-wheel and sang the air : " Il
ne revient pas ! . . . . ' which, after frequent
curtailments and restorations, has finally disappeared. All the same, this is one of the finest
pages of the entire score. The fact was that
prime donne regarded it as fatiguing and not
sufficiently effective !

Afterwards came Siebel, as at present, to console the poor abandoned girl. The annotations
point to music different from that with which
we are acquainted, and which would seem to be
preferable :

Les pleurs qui tom - bent de tes yeux! Les
pleurs qui tom - bent de vos yeux!

Marguerite entered the church ; then appeared
Valentin and a few soldiers singing " Déposons
les armes " and the scene continued with long
couplets by Valentin, responded to by the chorus.

These couplets were written, as evidenced by the
words, *fait-Sib.*, noted down by the author, but no
trace whatsoever remains of them. They have
been replaced by the popular chorus : " Gloire
immortelle de nos aieux " taken from the unfinished score of " Ivan le Terrible."

Valentin entered the house and Siebel the church
which, by a mechanical artifice that the huge stage
of the Théâtre-historique rendered possible, filled
up the entire available space and showed the in-
terior of the building. It was as accompaniment of
this impressive scenic effect that Gounod wrote
the orchestral prelude which precedes that of the

organ, a characteristic touch carrying us away from the emotions of the theatre and bringing us under those of the sanctuary by means so simple that it is impossible to admire them too much.

Berlioz, when dealing with the first performance of " Faust," made legitimate sport of a Mephistopheles retiring before the pommels of swords raised in the form of a cross, and yet showing no fear of a genuine cross by entering the church as he would a mill. In the " Faust " of Goethe, it is not Mephistopheles who torments Marguerite, it is an evil spirit. But at the Opéra, what was to be done ? Could a first-rate singer be confined to so short, and yet so important, a scene ? In one of the numerous avatars of the play there had been discovered a subterfuge. Marguerite did not enter the church ; just as she was crossing the threshold, she was stopped by Mephistopheles suddenly issuing from behind a pillar. This version did not last long ; the scene went back to the church, which it ought never to have left, and the public gave no sign of noticing the anomaly that had shocked Berlioz. This scene, however, sometimes preceding and at other times following the death of Valentin, went through many oscillations before settling once for all in its true place.

The chorus " Quand du Seigneur le jour luira "
is written in the libretto in C minor and bears the
annotation : " Transpose to F minor." The words
that follow admit of other music, which has not
been preserved :

Que di - rai - je a - lors au . . Sei - gneur ?

Où trou - ve - rai - je un pro - tec - teur, . .

Quand l'in - no - cent n'est pas sans peur !

accompanied by the same annotation, " in F
minor," which here is incomprehensible.

The " Nuit de Walpurgis " gave occasion for
many different attempts. I remember one rehearsal in which a band of figurants, cheaply
costumed as witches and riding their brooms,
leapt about like madmen showing their heavy
shoes and raising clouds of dust. There must also
have been a chorus of real witches, singing and
dancing round a cauldron filled with some blazing
liquid. We tread in Gounod's handwriting
" Grande ritournelle pour la chaudière." Ritor-
nello, cauldron, and witches have disappeared,
though afterwards, when the work was taken up

again, witches and cauldron reappeared at the end
of the Act. The words alone are given in the
libretto ; here is the music :

On another occasion Faust, in the presence " of
queens and courtezans," sang a drinking-song
which has disappeared without leaving behind
any regrets   In the original version, however,
just as, following the insinuation of Mephistopheles,
he was taking up a goblet, the phantom of Marguerite appeared before him, and Mephistopheles
thus accosted him :

ma - gie   et sor - ti - lè - - ge! ma -

- gie . et sor - ti - lè - ge!

ne va pas,   maî-tre fou, te laisser prendre au piè - ge!

When "Faust" was transferred to the stage
of the Opéra, everything pointed to the necessity
for introducing a ballet, a thing impossible at the
Théâtre Lyrique. Would it be believed that
Gounod suggested that I should write the music
of one ? At that time his religious ideas, he said,
forbade his undertaking such a task. The manner
in which I accepted his offer was a disguised
refusal. He understood, wrote the ballet himself,
and never had occasion to repent doing so.

The first evening, while the beautiful Marquet
in Grecian costume was evoking visions of Phidias
and Praxiteles, motionless women on each side
of the stage bore perfume-burning censers whence
issued streams of greyish-white smoke which was
wafted towards the spectators. The latter were

F

eagerly sniffing the delightful odour when a frightful smell, resembling that emitted by blue lights,
spread all over the theatre. . . .

The Prison Act began originally with Marguerite
as a mad woman, in a scene which has disappeared,
as has also the greater part of a long duet between
herself and Faust. No *prima donna* could have
endured the fatigue of such an Act, following immediately upon the others. Gounod told me that he
greatly regretted the mad scene, of which unfortunately he did not allow me to hear a note. No
other trace of this remains than the indication
'F sharp minor' in the composer's handwriting,
calculated to awaken a sense of keen regret, for
there is not a single *morceau* in the whole work
written in this key, with the exception of the
prelude of the Act, originally intended as the
preparation for this scene. Only this fragment
of the great duet remains :

Où sont les tor - tu - res, Les pleurs, les in -
- ju - res, la hon - te, l'ef - froi? . .
Tout a dis - pa - ru! te voi - là! c'est toi.

Later on, in the following passage :

Faust—Oui, mon cœur se souvient ! mais suis-moi !
　　l'heure presse ! . . .
Marguerite—Pourquoi détournes-tu les yeux ?
　　Embrassez-moi, Seigneur ! ou bien je vous
　　embrasse !

we find this modification, written by Gounod :

Faust—Oui, mon cœur est à toi ! mais suis-moi !
　　l'heure presse ! . . .
Marguerite—Non, reste encore ! et que ton bras
　　Comme autrefois au mien s'enlace !
Faust—Oh ciel ! Elle ne m'entend pas !

The work of Gounod's has achieved a glorious destiny, though the path of fame was not an easy one to follow. In contradistinction to certain works gradually launched on a successful career through judicious advertising, " Faust " was subjected, from its first appearance, to a degree of hostility which has never been relaxed. This fine production—at first not sufficiently Italian, then not sufficiently German, now regarded as too simple because it does not respond to that craze for exaggerated complication which is the bane of the new style of music, attaching prime importance to the human voice which it has become the fashion to disparage—has always had on its side the masses who do not trouble about theories, love to understand what they hear, and, when they see singers on the stage, naturally consider that they are there for the purpose of singing. The above-mentioned *brochure* of Soubies and Curzon establishes the fact that, in spite of a malevolent press, "Faust" has almost invariably attracted the crowds; inadequate receipts have been so infrequent that it is unnecessary to take them into consideration.

When "Faust" crossed Paris to find a new home at the Opéra, it was an event of importance. Everybody predicted a catastrophe. Some feared, others *hoped* that the music of Gounod, with its quiet and unobtrusive orchestra, would pale into insignificance by the side of the famous works which formed the basis of the repertory. The "Garden" Act, more particularly, would be literally annihilated on that immense stage. This Act of tender and delightful love-making just missed being omitted—at one time it was considered doubtful whether it should be altogether suppressed. The fear was expressed that it would not be *effective!*

Giving the lie to these evil predictions, it was found that the clear, simple, and yet delightfully coloured orchestral music of Gounod acquired its full value and importance in the large *salle*, bringing with it a charm it had not hitherto known.

How comes it that this lesson has not even yet been understood ? Why does one persist in resorting to sheer noise and parasitical complications which quite drown the human voice instead of sustaining and supporting it ?

The reason is that there are two kinds of simplicity. There is that of the simple-minded, of which it is unnecessary to speak, and there is another simplicity, which belongs to the highest consummation of art. But this latter it is not given to everyone to reach.

LISZT, THE PIANIST

THE hour of justice had struck when the centenary of Liszt's birth came round ; great festivals were organized and his works were performed on the grand scale. No longer was it possible to affirm that the author of " Christus," of the " Legend of Saint Elisabeth," of the Symphonies " Dante " and " Faust," and of the Symphonic Poems, was simply a writer of " pianists' music." We may now speak of the marvellous virtuoso without running the risk of doing injustice to this composer of genius.

Pianists' music ! Well, Mozart was the greatest pianist of his day, Beethoven was a pianist of the highest rank, and Sebastian Bach, that mighty genius, was an unrivalled organist and clavecinist.

Unfortunately for Liszt—an extraordinary performer who extracted from his instrument the strangest effects, completely transforming it as Paganini had transformed the violin—he was fated to emphasise his virtuosity.

All the same, it was not this virtuosity, however

amazing, but rather his own admirable musical nature that constituted his true worth. When accused of attaching undue importance to the pianoforte at the expense of the music, it was the contrary that really took place : his aim was to introduce the orchestra into the pianoforte. With wonderful ingenuity, substituting the free for the literal (and, therefore, unfaithful) translation, he actually succeeded in expressing on his instrument the sonorous measures of Beethoven's Symphonies and of Berlioz's " Symphonie Fantastique." Into his lesser pianoforte pieces (even the Fantasias which were written on opera motives) there enters the idea of the orchestra, giving an æsthetic character even to the most apparently futile things.

As most of his inventions have ceased to be copyright, in these days we are no longer aware of the radical transformation he wrought, of the many novel resources he introduced into pianoforte technique. A veritable revolution was effected, the sonority of the instrument appearing to have doubled in volume. To listen to some of his compositions from a distance, one would imagine that a duet rather than a solo was being played.

By new methods of fingering he opened up a wide field for those arabesque effects with which the pianoforte could not dispense, and which, before

his time, had had a very restricted field of action.
I say this without casting any reflection upon
Chopin, whose inventions along these lines have
been so valuable.

The part played by the left hand he developed to
an unusual degree. In the ancient pianoforte
music, each hand possesses its determinate rôle
from which it seldom departs : this is *dualist* music,
music in two elements.

In the quartet and the orchestra we have something additional ; here the musical structure com-
prises three elements : the song, the bass, and a
more or less complex intermediate part.

It was Liszt's wish to transfer this threefold
interest to the pianoforte, and he effected his object
by means of the left hand, directing it incessantly
from the low notes to the centre notes of the instrument. The left hand—poor thing !—was not
accustomed to such gymnastics, and to perform
these new duties it was compelled to acquire a
degree of suppleness and agility quite unusual. All
this did not take place without encountering oppo-
sition, of which no memory remains at the present
time. Certain of Liszt's compositions, which were
once regarded as impossible of execution, are now
everyday performances of the young pupils of the
Conservatoire. On the pianoforte, as on all other

instruments, virtuosity has made gigantic strides all along the line.

What hard things have been said against this virtuosity! How fiercely it has been attacked in the name of Art with a capital A! To think of that implacable, that impious war declared upon the Concertos both of Beethoven and of Mozart! One could not possibly have been more completely in the wrong.

In the first place—the fact must be proclaimed from the house-tops—in art a difficulty overcome is a thing of beauty. This truth has been affirmed by Théophile Gautier in immortal verse, and after such testimony there is nothing further to be said.

In the second place, virtuosity is a powerful aid to music, whose scope it extends enormously. It is because instrumentalists have all become virtuosi that Richard Wagner was enabled to dispense so lavishly that delightful wealth of sound, of which a good deal would have been impossible but for the virtuosity we affect to despise.

In such cases, however, beauty comes into existence only when the difficulty is really overcome to such a degree that the listener is unaware of its existence. We thus enter that realm of superior execution wherein Liszt was throned as a king, performing with the ease and assurance of a god.

Power and delicacy and charm, along with a rightly-accented rhythm were his, in addition to an unusual warmth of feeling, impeccable precision, and that gift of suggestion which creates great orators, the leaders and guides of the masses.

When interpreting the classics, he did not substitute his own personality for the author's, as do so many performers ; he seemed rather to endeavour to get at the heart of the music and find out its real meaning—a result sometimes missed even by the best of players.

This, moreover, was the plan he adopted in his transcriptions. The Fantasia on " Don Juan " sheds unexpected light upon the deeper meanings of Mozart's masterpiece.

Liszt left behind him admirable Études of a really terrifying nature, though most helpful in pianoforte work. He also wrote a " Method " which, imprudently entrusted to others whereas it ought never to have left the author's hands except to pass into the publisher's, has disappeared. The loss is irreparable. By this method most valuable teachings would have been handed down from generation to generation, combating those erroneous principles with which conscientious—though woefully mistaken—professors so lavishly flood the world.

Ah ! why have I not the art of word-painting ?

As I write I picture myself once again in the home of Gustave Doré, gazing upon that pallid face and those eyes that fascinated all listeners, whilst, beneath his apparently indifferent hands, in a wonderful variety of nuances, there moaned and wailed, murmured and roared the waves of the " Légende de Saint François de Paule marchant sur les flots " !

Never again will there be seen or heard anything to equal it.

THE FALSE MASTERPIECES OF MUSIC

MANY readers, on seeing the title of this article, will imagine that it is my intention to support the demolishers of the past. This is by no means the case ; respectful of the past, I can even respect the dead. Not without a feeling of involuntary veneration do I turn over the pages of these old scores, once the objects of so much fame and glory, though now plunged in eternal oblivion. In certain parts there is still about them an uncommon degree of majesty. Moreover, are we certain that the works which at present fill *us* with enthusiasm will retain all their prestige as time goes on ? Who can tell what will be said of them a century hence ? The most eulogistic commentators of the present day do not surpass what the *literati* of their age wrote on " Moses " and " Semiramis." In them new worlds were discovered ; but then, it was added, the French are not sufficiently *sensitive* to understand such music : of that the Italians alone are capable !

Rossini, with mournful smile, saw the public

gradually cease to take an interest in his operas. When the suggestion of giving " Semiramis " at the Opéra was made, he wrote a letter in which he disclaimed all responsibility. " This work," he said, " was written for a public and for singers who no longer exist." He allowed the proposition to be carried into effect so that his old friend Carafa might receive author's rights, it being his task to supervise the performance, though Rossini himself refused to be present.

Youth is ever inclined for war : on many occasions has it attacked immortal masterpieces, like the little mad-headed serpent of the fable. The futile assault upon Racine by the romanticists of 1830 is not yet forgotten. Vacquerie, who had written " What have I against Phèdre ? The dragonnades of the Cevennes ! " thus arbitrarily confusing quite different sets of ideas, made way for Racine towards the end of his life. More recently we have seen scorn poured upon the heads of Lamartine, Hugo, and Musset, though no harm to them seems to have resulted. In music, when they began to fight " for the good cause," they imagined it their duty to wage upon Mozart a war with which, from the outset, I deliberately refused to associate myself. The cloud is now past, and the star of Mozart shines more brilliantly than ever.

There are some who attack Beethoven's Ninth Symphony. The *Finale*, in which the gaiety of the gods insolently bursts forth, would appear to lack distinction in the opinion of certain persons who confuse " distinction " with " a distinguished air." In vain will they try to sully the purity of this diamond. Other works are more assailable, though there is every reason why they should be respected. It will not be easy to induce me to believe that music could have delighted or thrilled generation after generation unless it possessed the true ring. This is easy to recognise, by the way, if we will take the trouble to study it, and not judge by degenerate performances which stultify it.

This is not what I mean by the " false masterpieces of music." I refer to pieces, either ridiculous or mediocre, which the masses have thought they were compelled to admire, falling headlong into the snares set for them by publishers of too knavish a type.

First, there were the " Waltzes " of Beethoven. These were authentic, written by the author in his youth ; slight, insignificant *morceaux* devoid of charm, in no way resembling the modern idea of the waltz, but simply a three-time rhythm.

This vogue appeared at a time when, the Conservatoire concerts having begun a series of per_ formances of the Symphonies, it became a matter of *bon ton* to appear to admire Beethoven. The publisher of the " Waltzes " supplied these admirers —hungry enough, though of feeble digestion—with such nourishment as they were able to swallow. He had cleverly placed at the head of the collection the delightful " Désir " of Schubert, naturally attributed to Beethoven. All these waltzes were played very slowly, with an excessively affected expression, contrasting in the most ridiculous manner with the vapid platitude of the music.

About the same time, Weber's " Dernière Pensée " (known in England as " Weber's Last Waltz ") was at the height of its popularity. Here is the story of this spurious composition :

A German company had performed the " Freischütz " at Paris with great success ; in the salons, Liszt had played the " Invitation à la Valse." Weber was in the fashion. Then a publisher took a waltz of Reissiger, a composer unknown in France, and made of it the " dernière pensée " of the composer who died in the prime of life. By playing this *morceau* slowly and with many nuances, being very careful to perform with one hand after the other in accordance with the strict principles of bad playing, holding the head on one side and raising the eyes to heaven, melomaniac women of romantic disposition converted the piece into something very affecting to ears of the Midas type. I was a child at the time, and completely ignorant of music as of everything else. All the same, my instinct rebelled, and I remained cold when listening both to Beethoven's Waltzes and to Weber's " Dernière Pensée " ; all that I felt was a sense of the most profound boredom.

There is another mystification that has been more dangerous, for it has lasted until now—Schubert's " Lebewohl " (" Farewell ").

Schubert's first " Lieder," when imported into France, were a revelation. As is well known, instead of being a simple accompaniment intended to support the voice, they united for the first time —to my knowledge, at all events—the melodic charm of the vocal part with an interesting and strongly emphasised pianoforte part. These diversified accompaniments being impossible of execution by unskilful or immature players, a publisher came to their assistance by bringing out under Schubert's name a " Lied " composed by von Weihrauch, an amateur. The *morceau*, being well written, did no dishonour to Schubert's name, but if it is closely examined a great difference between the two composers is seen in the banal simplicity of the accompaniment, and in the melodic poverty of the cantus which repeats the same note a dozen times. The success of the " Lebewohl " was very great, owing largely to an extreme facility of execution which the authentic works did not present ; moreover, the song dealt with the immortality of the soul :

> La mort est une amie
> Qui rend la liberté ;
> Au ciel reçois la vie
> Et pour l'éternité !

When a superbly-built woman, gifted with a splendid voice, sang these words which ended in a succession of formidable chest notes, the effect was irresistible.

The colossal success of the " Lebewohl " reached the ears of the true author. It was perfectly reasonable than von Weihrauch should loudly protest and claim his rights. Vain, however, were his efforts ! The " Lebewohl " was Schubert's so far as the public was concerned, and it will remain so for all time. Many an amateur has spoken enthusiastically of Schubert, though the only thing of his that he knew was this " Lebewohl."

The strangest of these bogus works is, perhaps, the one of which Victor Hugo was a victim. Whose idea was it to give him—as emanating from Beethoven—a nondescript melody taken, it would appear, from a " Revue des Variétés " ? Diligent

G

investigators might, perhaps, succeed in discovering the author of this marvel. Utterly ignorant of music, as is well known, Victor Hugo readily swallowed the enticing bait. He was induced to write some lines for this " admirable musique," to present the world with the spectacle of a collaboration between the great French genius and the great German genius. He wrote " Stella," which agrees neither in character nor in prosody with the following somewhat bizarre melody :

The ninth bar is superfluous ; it breaks up the

phrase and produces an effect similar to that of a
line which contains thirteen feet.

Hugo doted on this air, and had it played for him
every evening by Madame Drouet.   When the idea
came to me to write a " Hymne à Victor Hugo,"
thinking to produce something special for the poet,
I undertook to give a musical turn to this legendary
melody.   By suppressing the parasitic bar, presenting the theme in a certain way :

superposing two fragments of the melody :

in a word, by applying all the tricks of the trade, I succeeded in obtaining from this artificial diamond a few flashes. . . .

So true is it that " the trade " is not without its uses ! There are some who disdain it, and acknowledge nothing but inspiration. Inspiration is the priceless and indispensable material, the rough diamond, the virgin metal ; " the trade " is the art of the lapidary and the jeweller : it is equivalent to saying that it is Art itself. Those who despise " the trade " will never be more than amateurs.

A NOTE ON RAMEAU

RAMEAU, the greatest French composer of the
18th century, whose works held so important a
place on the stage, had become almost forgotten
in the 20th. A few pieces for the clavecin and the
delightful chorus, " En ces doux asiles," were almost
all that anyone knew of him, for practically the
whole of his work had remained unpublished.

This injustice has now come to an end, thanks to
Durand, who undertook the gigantic task of
publishing the complete works of this marvellous
genius, the contemporary and rival of Sebastian
Bach. Not that he possesses Bach's supreme
elegance and wonderful fecundity of production,
for his style is uneven and *gauche*, and occasionally
disconcerting; nevertheless, the *gaucherie* and in-
accuracy are not the work of an unskilful artist.
As a matter of fact, they are something quite
different; it might be said that in the progress of
the various parts he works in obedience to special
laws that are independent of the requirements

89

of the ear. His superiority is along other lines,
e.g., in his genius for dramatic effect, and in a
profundity of knowledge which has enabled him
to work out a musical system and to make sur-
prising discoveries in the realm of harmony. He
holds supreme sway in the theatre just as Bach
does in the church. The reason they are both
mentioned in the same breath is because they
are so totally different from each other.

Some years ago an attempt was made to restore
his works to the stage ; the result has not been
what was anticipated. It must, however, be
acknowledged at once that this was not the fault
of the composer, the interpreter, or the public.
This does not prove that the resurrection is impossible, failure being due to difficulties that had
not been suspected.

These are of various kinds. The first we en-
counter is owing to the fact that the pitch in the
17th and 18th centuries was a tone lower than it
is at the present time. The old organs, even as
they were in my own youth, left no doubt whatever
on this point. The strange thing is that this low
pitch existed in France alone ; the works of
Handel, Bach, Mozart, and the Italian scores of
Gluck, in their mode of dealing with the human
voice, show nothing which would lead us to suppose

the pitch very different from our own ; and yet
no sooner do we examine a French score than we
find ourselves confronted with music that it is
impossible to sing.

Whereas everywhere else the four usual parts of
the chorus were divided, half and half, for male
and female voices—soprano, contralto, tenor, bass
—in the French scores all the female voices are
united in the treble, sometimes divided into firsts
and seconds ; the other three parts, *haute-contre*,
taille, and bass are male voices. The *hautes-
contre* are first tenors ; the *tailles* are second tenors
and baritones. These first tenor parts, however,
soar to inaccessible heights ; it has even been
thought that the *hautes-contre* were special voices
which are no longer to be heard. If this part is
entrusted to tenors, we have, as the result, in-
tolerable screams and cries. Sung by contraltos,
all its dash and brilliancy depart and it loses whatever value it possessed.

As a matter of fact, in interpreting this music
as it is written we find that it has been transposed
a note higher. The voices, when not transposed
out of their range, find themselves badly placed ;
the singers, in a state of perpetual inconvenience
and constraint, are unable to give their parts the
true accent or to pronounce the words distinctly

—a matter absolutely indispensable in works where declamation is of such importance.

Consequently, we must resign ourselves to transposition. Now, this is not so easy as might be imagined ; it is really very delicate work. Moreover, even in the case of transposition, the *hautes-contre* are still occasionally too sharp ; this is due to the fact that in those days they sang *en voix blanche*, an emission of sound which greatly facilitates the attack of high notes, though the voice thereby acquires a timbre similar to that of street cries, one which our modern ears would not tolerate for a moment. In certain cases, then, recourse must be had to the use of female voices. This I have effected in two admirable Psaumes of Rameau, which are thus made suitable for concert performance.

This, however, is nothing compared with the work of interpretation, strictly so called. In these days music is written almost exactly as it should be performed. In the past such was not the case, use being made of conventional signs which had to be translated. When performing ancient music as it is written, we are like a man spelling out the words of a foreign language which he is unable to pronounce.

Apparently the greatest difficulty is connected

with the *appoggiatura*, which is not used nowadays. Each one interprets it as he pleases, after
his own taste. Now, this is not a matter of taste,
but rather of erudition ; the question before us
is not to know what we prefer but what the author
intended to write. The key of the mystery lies
in the violin method of Mozart *père*. In the
library of the Conservatoire there are three editions ;
the oldest is the correct one. We are greatly
amazed when we note the difference between the
written sign and its true interpretation. At one
of the Conservatoire concerts, having to play
the D minor Concerto of Mozart, I was considerably
puzzled over the bar :

and was not a little surprised to discover that it had
to be translated thus :

On other occasions, the *appoggiatura* should
resolve into a rest, which is then replaced by a note.
It will be seen, in the example quoted, that the
final quaver, when played, becomes a semiquaver.

The reason of this is that, in former times, the " arithmetical " value of the notes was not taken into account as it is nowadays ; a breve was a breve, devoid of any precise value. Moreover, whenever in Handel or in Rameau we find this rhythm :

it should be translated thus :

This rhythm is met with very frequently, especially in Handel.

Finally, there are innumerable signs the interpretation of which is occasionally impossible, all contemporary methods indicating that they cannot be described, and that to perform them one must have heard them sung by a professor. Fortunately, in all probability these embellishments were not indispensable ; they appeared in such profusion owing to the prevalent bad taste of the times, and we need not regret their disappearance.

One thing more, however. A close study of these works has convinced me that the values of the vocal parts are approximate, and that we must take into consideration, declamation, not notation, if we are to interpret the melody part, and not merely the recitative, in accordance with the real intention of the composer.

The composer himself seems to have delighted in piling up difficulties by continually changing the tempo ; two-, three-, and four-time incessantly follow one another, and the two-time measure has to be twice as rapid as the four-time.

It is impossible for players to find their way creditably out of this labyrinth ; preliminary study is needed if any practical result is to be attained.

Shall I speak of the instruments ? These do not offer any considerable variety. The habit of accompanying the recitative on the clavecin, which might be tolerable in a small hall, has become impossible in a large one for audiences accustomed to the powerful sonorities of the present day. The orchestra of old was made up quite differently from the present orchestra : several flutes, oboes, and bassoons, an occasional horn and trumpet. This could not have been very harmonious. Modern orchestration, effected with the requisite taste and discretion, similar to that with which Mozart enriched " The Messiah " and " Alexander's Feast," would assuredly make these works more attractive, if not more valuable. All the same, a very respectful and a very light pen would be essential to the task.

The difficulties are great, though not insurmountable, and we may hope that the day will come when the music of Rameau, regarded in its true light, will no longer be confined to the erudite, but will be acclaimed by the masses.

A CHOPIN M.S.

THE F MAJOR BALLADE IN THE MAKING

THIS manuscript* is written on thin fragile paper of moderate dimensions, 11″ x 9″. Evidently it was so fragile that erasure was impossible : consequently, whenever Chopin changed his mind, he made his corrections so extremely close that the originals at first appear to have utterly disappeared. And yet, with the aid of a magnifying glass and a fair stock of patience, it has been possible to bring to light the greater part of what was originally written.

From the very outset we find a certain hesitancy, as though the author were feeling his way.

He had written :

The first two notes † † have disappeared.

* Recently presented by M. Saint-Saëns to the Library of the Paris *Conservatoire*. (Translator's Note.)

At the 7th bar, instead of

the author had first written

At the 39th bar < > the line < has been
suppressed

At the 3rd, 7th, and 15th bars of the *Presto con
fuoco* the figured passages :

have given place to these :

A little farther on, in the series of chords :

an obliterated above the G seems to point

to the author's first intention to write the chord

Again taking up the first motive (First Tempo),
the hesitancy becomes more pronounced than at
the beginning.

The author first wrote

then

and finally

At the 6th bar of this first Tempo, the passage :

ran thus originally :

At the 23rd bar of the first Tempo, we find

which was simplified as follows :

At the following presto, 3rd bar

13th bar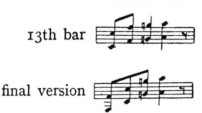

final version

At the bar preceded by a double stroke and with a

natural at the clef : the manuscript bears

the indication *Agitato*.

This indication is valuable : it enables us to break the rhythm and thus diminish the extreme difficulty of the final period.

With the object of lessening this difficulty, the author, who had at first written :

simplified the passage thus :

All the same, the difficulty remains so manifest that Chopin himself only on rare occasions played

H

this Ballade. Madame Viardot told me that he had
often played for her the Andantino of the beginning,
but he had never continued and finished the piece.
He played this Andantino without any nuance
whatsoever, with the exception of the two indicated
and these he strongly accented.

At the 6th bar of the Agitato, the bass which at
first was written

became

The 11th and 12th bars :

and the 15th and 16th :

had originally been :

A little farther on (17-18),

gave place to :

We now come to the most interesting part of the manuscript.

At the 21st and 22nd, 25th and 26th bars of the *Agitato*, we have the fine passages in the bass,

which were modified as follows :

Possibly some purist dropped a hint to Chopin

that the left hand did not accord correctly with the
right hand, a matter which, however, in a rapid
movement like this, was no drawback at all.

The figure  had never

satisfied me, though I could not tell why.   I understood the reason when I read the manuscript and
ascertained that the author had made a regrettable
correction.

For the last three bars, the author had originally
written :

and afterwards :

The printed copy gives

the definite version certainly intended by the author.

This manuscript shows us with what reserve Chopin used the pedal ; in several passages where he had indicated it, it was afterwards suppressed. The reason it is frequently indicated in his works is that he did not wish it to be used when not indicated. To dispense with this help is no easy matter ; for many it would even be impossible, so general has the abuse of the pedal become. To play without the pedal calls for a degree of suppleness in the hands, of which not every one, however talented, is capable.

PART II

HÉLÈNE

LONG had I had the vision of Helen fleeing into the night, arriving crushed, all her strength gone, at the sea-side far from her palace, rejoined by Paris, the scene of passion, the resistance finally overcome, the last flight of the two lovers after a desperate struggle. . . . .

For never could I look upon Helen simply as a woman in love ; she was the sport of Destiny, the victim of Aphrodite offered up by the goddess to her own glory, the prize of the Golden Apple, a great figure whose sin excites no mockery but rather a kind of sacred terror. See her on the walls of Ilion, the city upon which her very presence summons ruin and massacre. When she passes, the old men of Troy rise and greet her. Later on we find her in her husband's house, doing the honours of his palace with queenly dignity. No one dreams of reproaching her for the past, for leaving home, for the years spent in Troy and the many Greeks dead on her account! The daughter of Zeus meets with naught but universal regard and respect.

Consequently I had conceived the idea of depicting in music the *hegira* of the two lovers, had it not been so well known how successfully this idea was parodied. To have these two epic characters, that had become comic, taken seriously, was for a long time not to be thought of ; I had put off my plan, and, with the lapse of years, the very project itself had been forgotten.

A request made by M. Gunsbourg—which I at first rejected though afterwards he insisted upon my considering it carefully—sufficed to bring it all back again and to present Helen and Paris before me more living than ever.

My first intention—the intention of an idle man, I grant you—was to find some one who would collaborate with me. But who should this be ? A collaborator might have wished to add his ideas on to my own and so ruin the simplicity of my conception, the result being that I made up my mind to work alone.

Alone ? Not altogether. Following the example of our classical writers I had enlisted the services of Homer, Theocritus, Aeschylus, Vergil and even Ovid.

Without the help of Vergil should I have has-
arded that description of Priam's palace, those
gilded roofs and walls lined with shining polished
brass, adorned with dazzling statues which in all
probability were polychrome, that *ensemble* which
gives almost a sense of verisimilitude to the strange
architecture of Gustave Moreau ? Should I have
dared to utter the line :

> Dans le sang de ses fils Priam est égorgé ?

*   *   *   *   *   *   *

Having made my notes and outlined my scenario,
all I had to do was to set to work. At the time, I
was in Cairo, the guest of His Highness Mohammed
Ali, Pasha of Egypt, the Khedive's brother. I was
in the enjoyment of complete liberty and of a
calm undisturbed by visitors. These had probably been scared away by the guard of the palace
gate, huge fellows in gorgeous costumes and
formidably armed.

I cannot possibly say how I found the first
musical phrase to which I subsequently adapted
the line :

> Des astres de la nuit tes yeux ont la clarté !

I had reached this point when the director
of the Khedive's theatre conceived the idea of
giving a grand concert on behalf of the sailors of

Brittany and of composing it entirely from my works.

Suddenly I found myself plunged into a round of rehearsals, compelled to take my own part in this solemnity. All this was incompatible with work that was in its initial critical stage. Regretfully I gave up " Hélène," and when, later on, I wished to take it up again, it was quite impossible. I was bewildered, out of tune so to speak. I had to quit my delightful abode in Cairo and proceed to the middle of the desert into the Thebaid of Ismailia—a refuge of light and silence—for what one is pleased to call " inspiration."

Ismailia, the favourite sojourn of the Prince of Arenberg, is a heavenly spot. It is a *beata solitudo* inhabited by a number of highly civilised people of both sexes employed by the Suez Canal administration, a small though choice colony which included poets of no mean talent ! And as these kindly folk are very busy, they people the solitude without disturbing it.

In twelve days I had written my poem. Then I set sail at Port Said for Paris, where preparations were in progress for a revival of " Henry VIII." at the Opéra. Once this was over, I was quite tired out ; my " composing machine " would not work any longer and I needed a week at Biarritz

and another at Cannes to recover. Then I re-
membered that Aix-en-Savoie was close to a
flower-decked mountain, surrounded by a wonderful panorama and easy of access. Soon I found
myself installed on Mount Revard where I sketched
out almost the whole of the music of " Hélène "
to be completed subsequently in Paris.

It is thus that one should always work, in calm
and silence, far from importunate visitors and
distractions of various kinds, soothed by the
glorious sights of nature and the odours of flowers.
When this is possible, work is more than a pleasure,
it is voluptuous delight.

There has been noticed a certain analogy between the appearance of Pallas in " Hélène "
and that of Brünnhilde in the Second Act of the
" Walküre." Of this fact I was aware, though
I found it impossible to avoid it.

Helen appeals for help to Zeus, her father.
What can he do ? Come himself ? So formidable
an appearance would not fit in with the framework
of the opera. Send Mercury his messenger to
her ? The ancients might have permitted this,
for Mercury conducted souls to the infernal regions;
though in our opinion Hermes is not a god to be
taken seriously, we cannot imagine him as threatening or terrible, predicting a catastrophe. On

the contrary, such a rôle fell naturally to Pallas, the living antithesis of Cytherea who was also a daughter of Zeus ; consequently hesitation was impossible.

In art, when logic commands, it must be obeyed and nothing else must be considered. Assuredly it is vexatious to find oneself in disaccord with one of the finest scenes on any stage ; it would be even more vexatious to withdraw before an analogy which was necessarily inevitable.

Helen and Paris, Samson and Delilah, Adam and Eve, drama is always the same in its essence : the triumphant temptation, the irresistible attraction of the forbidden fruit.

Though protesting for form's sake, we have any amount of indulgence for and even sympathy with the vanquished.

Even the Church rejoices over Adam's lapse. *O felix culpa!* which had made necessary the Redemption, the very foundation of the Christian religion.

Suppose Helen and Paris, terrified by the predictions of Pallas, were to bid each other an eternal farewell, they would enlist our esteem but would interest us no more. Who ever took any interest in Menelaus ?

This situation, which can be carried back to the

Garden of Eden, is of a disquieting nature ; it
contains a problem which no one so far has succeeded in solving. It may be that the civilisa-
tion of which we are so proud, young enough in
comparison with the age of humanity, is but
transitory, a progress towards a higher state wherein that which now seems obscure will become
clear, and certain things that appear to us essential
will be nothing but words. Let us hope it will be
so. As Carmen, that other incarnation of the same
idea, says, it is always our privilege to hope.

SARASATE

YEARS have now passed since there once called upon me Pablo de Sarasate, youthful and fresh-looking as the spring, and already a celebrity, though a dawning moustache had only just begun to appear. He had been good enough to ask me, in the most casual way imaginable, to write a concerto for him. Greatly flattered and delighted at the request, I gave him a promise and kept my word with the *Concerto in A Major* to which— I do not know why—the German title of *Concertstück* has been given. Subsequently I wrote for him a *Rondo capricioso* in the Spanish style and later on the *Concerto in B Minor*. During the composition of this Concerto he gave me valuable advice to which is certainly due the considerable degree of favour it has met with on the part of violinists themselves.

Those who were in the habit of attending my Monday musical soirées have not forgotten the brilliant effect produced by my illustrious friend.

This was so markedly the case that for several years afterwards no violinists could be prevailed upon to perform at my house, so terrified were they at the idea of inviting comparison. Nor did he shine by reason of his talent alone, but also because of his brilliant intellect and the inexhaustible animation of his conversation which was invariably interesting and suggestive.

By playing my compositions throughout the world on his magic instrument, Pablo de Sarasate has done me the greatest possible service, and I am pleased to have the opportunity of paying him publicly the tribute of my admiration and gratitude, and of a friendship which follows him beyond the tomb.

MUSICAL DIGRESSIONS.

OPINIONS on art—especially on musical art—
have at all times been liable to strange aberrations. Art inspires a wealth of suggestion ; along
this line of thought, chalk can easily be passed
off as cheese. The public willingly allows itself
to be gulled. On perusing once again what
Stendhal said of Cimarosa, what Balzac said
of Rossini, one is amazed at the judgments they
passed on their contemporaries. The latter listened
with gaping mouths, imagining in their simplicity
that the reason they did not find in this Italian
music everything it was desired to make them
see was that they were incapable of understanding
it.

Fifty years ago, one dared not express a doubt
as to the value of famous operas which nowadays
it is the fashion to regard as devoid of melody, of
harmony, of instrumentation, of everything. At
that time, Beethoven, the divine Beethoven, was
the unknown quantity in music. Do not think

that I am making up all this ; one does not invent such things.

Without, therefore, making useless personal allusions, let us not exhibit amazement at certain judgments ; here, as elsewhere, there is nothing new under the sun. May we not, however, warn sincere readers and put them on their guard against the assertions of certain persons, doubtless of the utmost good faith, though excessively liable to suggestion ? It may be divined that I am alluding to those, well known to be a numerous band, who flock to the banner of the mighty Richard, and beneath its shade engage in a fight that has long been inconclusive.

They are not content that their god should triumph ; there must even be victims sacrificed on his altars.

Mendelssohn first of all. Certainly there is lack of uniformity in his work. But what of " Elijah," the " Midsummer Night's Dream," the sonatas for the organ, the preludes and fugues for the pianoforte, the Scottish Symphony, the Reformation Symphony ? . . . Try to accomplish a like task !

They would have us believe that when he first appeared he was accepted without a struggle, his " mediocrity " having at the outset placed him on a level with the masses.

Do not believe anything of the kind.

I was present at the very first performance of the " Midsummer Night's Dream " and of the Symphonies, given before a Parisian public, and I still remember that I broke more than one lance in his defence. At the first performances of the " Midsummer Night's Dream" I saw old *habitués* of the Conservatoire holding their heads in their hands as they asked in tones of anguish why the Société des Concerts inflicted such horrors on its subscribers. . . . Only by degrees did this public discover the Berceuse, then the Scherzo, then the Marche, then the Agitato, and finally the Overture. It was a tedious process !

Another victim : Meyerbeer. It was mainly against his " Huguenots " that an outcry was raised, by reason of its popular and long unchallenged success. Robert Schumann lent powerful aid in this direction through an article he wrote which declared that the " Huguenots " was not " music."

Unfortunately, when Schumann applied his marvellous talent to opera, he created " Geneviève." Now, " Geneviève " is assuredly charming music, though of a kind ill adapted to the theatre. Henceforth, so far as the " Huguenots " is concerned, Schumann's judgment is lacking in authority. On

I

the other hand, we have the opinion of Berlioz—who is known to be anything but indulgent in criticism—and he in his famous " Traité d'Instrumentation " quotes fragments of the great duo, " cette scène immortelle." This, in my opinion, is praise of no negligible kind.

      *   *   *   *   *   *   *

Immolated victims ! We must act in such fashion that the god be right in everything (otherwise he would no longer be a god) ; we must recognise not only the many dazzling qualities he possesses but also those he lacks.

For instance, his clarity will be extolled, as also his wealth of melody. Certainly, he is clear whenever he wishes to be, just as certain women are virtuous when it pleases them ; though they are not the ones whose virtue one is in the habit of praising. It is not in Helen but in Penelope that virtue is extolled ; it is in Mozart that clarity is personified, not in Wagner.

Apologists have gone so far as to claim that there is no difficulty which the orchestra cannot overcome in the Bayreuth *répertoire*, and that the latter does not even contain any *gaucheries ;* though certain passages are not only difficult or *gauches,* but quite impossible of execution.

I have before me a very interesting and well-written article on " The Future of the Lyrical Drama." In it the author has criticised kings, heroes, gods, rich costumes, everything legendary or mysterious, the almost universal disposition to place the action in far-away lands and far-distant times. As I read, I was afraid I might be proceeding in the direction of a negation of Wagner's work, for it had always appeared to me that this dealt with gods and heroes, legends and mysteries, and that whenever the author decided to venture into real life, he had had recourse to the costumes and the customs of antiquity.

Such was not the case. Siegfried's forge, the shoes of Hans Sachs suffice to make the " Tetralogy " and the " Meistersingers " realistic works. Do not, however, imagine that Wagner is capable of coarse realism ! Like Beethoven, he repudiates the direct imitation of nature ; he does not imitate the sound of the iron, he substitutes the man for the thing, the smith for his tool, expressive art for pure imitation. The author dwells on this at considerable length.

This is all very fine, but it is not true. An anvil—a real anvil—part exists in the orchestra, written in the score. The effects obtained by Wagner are very picturesque, and if he has not substituted " expressive art for pure imitation, the smith for his tool," I humbly confess I will not take exception to it. In the " Rheingold," too, he has introduced an entire orchestra of anvils, large, middle-sized, and small, which clang away for some considerable time. They strike *crescendo* whilst the orchestra is gradually dying away, and continue all alone for a few bars, afterwards continuing *decrescendo* whilst the orchestra gradually resumes its proper rôle ; their appearance and their disappearance blend in the ensemble. The effect is original and striking in the extreme. I heard it for the first time in Munich, at the performance organised by command of Ludwig the Third, against the wish of the author himself, who refused to put in an appearance. The anvil solo passage caused a sense of giddiness in the listener, and no doubt this was displeasing to Wagner when he heard it at Bayreuth, for he suppressed it during the rehearsals. I regretted this, as I have always missed the castanets that were originally played to a trimetrical rhythm on resuming the Bacchanale motive in " Tannhäuser." They too have been discontinued.

Gods and heroes, far-off lands and bygone times : all this is unquestionably very useful in lyrical drama, but not indispensable, as M. Charpentier has triumphantly demonstrated in " Louise." But

M. Charpentier, like the true man of the theatre
he is, has diverted the difficulty in all sorts of ingenious ways ; he has even transported us right
into faëry-land in his vision of an illuminated Paris
as seen from the heights of Montmartre.

To return to what we were saying, can we not
see things as they really are ?   What aberration is
it that makes us delight in erroneous reasoning
when we can reason correctly, as is possible in the
case of those I have mentioned ?   One of them
may well say : " In its essence, art does not change ;
men only change their minds as to its methods
and its limitations. Once they become certain
that these latter are purely arbitrary and that
everything in the realm of the beautiful has a right
to live, they will the more easily conceive of the
inexhaustible fecundity of art."

Let us think over these noble words, and desire—
though without expecting it—that they may be
rightly read and valued, and may serve as a guide
for future judgments.

THE METRONOME

Music differs from the plastic arts in that the element in which the latter work is division of space, whereas that in which music works is division of time.

In reality, music is the art of combining sounds simultaneously (harmony) or successively (melody). In either case, a sound being composed of a certain number of isochronous vibrations in a given time, the whole of music is reduced to a relation between numbers. Melody and harmony are nothing else than rhythmical combinations.

Sounds may be regarded, first, from the standpoint of the greater or less rapidity of the vibrations of which they are composed, and secondly, from the standpoint of their duration. In both cases, the relation between the different sounds alone constitutes the entire musical interest. In the fifteenth and sixteenth centuries, no one troubled about anything else. The pitch was arbitrary, and so no indication whatsoever guided the musician as to the rapidity or the slowness of the execution in what is called the " movement " of a *morceau*.

The development of the art of singing, by appealing to all the resources of the voice and to the entire range of the vocal scale, has gradually made perceptible the necessity of an absolute point of departure regarding pitch ; each country chooses its own just as it pleases.

Art, in the pursuit of its own line of evolution, came to recognise the necessity of one single pitch, and the *Académie des Sciences* solved the problem by creating the normal pitch which the other nations adopted in turn.

Again, the development of rhythmical combinations produced the necessity of determining the movement of musical pieces. This was done in vague terms which each one interpreted as he could, nor was any other means known until the appearance of the metronome, a timepiece supplied with a cursor index and a graduated scale based on the division of the minute of time, and invented at the end of the eighteenth century by Maelzel.

In the most frequently used metronomes, the divisions range from the one-fortieth to the one-two hundred and eighth of a minute.

This instrument, now seen everywhere, can unfortunately only be of real use on condition it is an instrument *de précision*, which is not always the case. In the past there have been too many badly constructed and falsely regulated metronomes which have led musicians astray instead of guiding them.

The *Académie des Sciences*, which has done such good service to the musical art by creating the normal pitch, might well endow music with a normal and mathematically regulated metronome, and induce the Government to see to it that all such instruments, before being sold to the public, should be tested and stamped, as is the case with weights and measures.

OBSERVATIONS OF A FRIEND OF
ANIMALS

ONE day, when speaking in the *Chambre*, Monseigneur Dupanloup, doubtless imagining himself in the pulpit, was thundering against the vices and abominations of the age. Amongst the impious propositions he handed over to public indignation was the following :

Il y a des animaux qui réfléchissent.

An imprudent phrase, a defect in the armour which it would have been better not to expose to view ! For, were it necessary to the spiritualistic theory that animals should be incapable of reflection, then it would indeed be in a very bad way. Since the sermon of the " fougueux prélat," as he was called, there have been innumerable investigations into the intelligence of animals, and this latter has been proved with such wealth of evidence that only those who deliberately shut their eyes refuse to believe it. We are not now living in the days when Madame de Grignan, under Descartes' influence, refused the offer of a pretty little dog under the pretext that she did not wish "s'embarrasser de semblables machines." Machines, these poor little animals, so devoted and affectionate !

Let me say at once that my ideas are neither spiritualistic nor materialistic ; on this question I once wrote an essay entitled : *Problèmes et Mystères*, in the Nouvelle Revue. These are matters of which I know but little, as they do not come within my special domain. And I lack the authority of an expert.

These hypotheses are based on the fact that the words " matter " and " spirit " are given to simple phenomena whose cause is unknown, and psychic phenomena begin with what is called living matter. Psychic comes from ψυχή soul, but soul distinct from matter cannot enter into this category ; all the same, we have to use the word " psychic " in default of another which it is unnecessary to coin since everybody knows quite well what we are dealing with.

Now, my opinion is that psychic phenomena form a long chain, an ensemble that may be compared to the solar spectrum, with instinct at one extremity and intelligence at the other ; an ensemble which no living being would seem to possess in its completeness. There is agreement in no longer regarding instinct and intelligence as two irreducible entities, and the word " unconscious " has been substituted for the world " instinct," it being recognised that the unconscious plays a large part in human nature. As we gradually depart from the human position, we find that instinct gains in extent what intelligence loses and in many cases it penetrates into regions which intelligence could not enter : in the insect world it even arrives at results we cannot understand. But, just as in the most intelligent man, instinct, although degenerate, is far from having wholly disappeared, so in those animals whose instinct is most highly developed, undeniable flashes of intelligence appear. We must go right down to the amœba, to the vegetable world, to find instinct free of all trace of intelligence : so at least it appears to me ! and perhaps in millions of years, if the earth is then still inhabitable, there will appear under new conditions of existence a being of pure and fully conscious intelligence.

The signs of intelligence afforded by animals have interested me from my earliest childhood. I will now relate a few of my observations.

* * * * * * *

Although zoologically the spider is not an insect,

I will place it in this category—with which it is connected—for greater convenience.

In spite of the admiration one must feel for its work, the spider has always filled me with a sense of invincible horror. In the hope of overcoming this troublesome aversion I have from time to time tamed one of these small animals. A certain amount of patience is needed. At the first attempts, the terrified spider drops to the end of its thread or else quickly hides away. After three or four days, it begins to feel reassured, but an entire week is needed, after cunningly graduated experiments, before it will take a fly from the finger of the observer. By this time it has lost all fear. Mention has elsewhere been made of the spider's taste for music ; this I have frequently noticed out in the country when playing the piano. Quite against my will I attracted huge spiders whose vicinity was anything but pleasant to me.

The most curious sign of intelligence was afforded me by the spiders of Cochin China. In that country, spiders of enormous size, not at all terrifying seeing that they are never visible except from a distance, stretch horizontal and parallel lines to a relatively considerable distance from one tree to another. From these webs they hang, head downwards. Now, when the French on occupying the country set up telegraph wires, these little insects, finding a warp ready made, took advantage of the situation ; they established themselves on these wires which spared them the greater part of their task, and contented themselves with spinning the woof on which they watched for their prey.   It is difficult not to regard this fact as the result of observation and reflection.

*   *   *   *   *   *   *

A great deal has been said regarding ants, their activities and their combats.   I will not go into this subject but will simply relate an experience I had which shows that in ants as in men there are differences of temperament and character.

I was in the forest of Fontainebleau, watching half a dozen ants feasting upon the excrement of a squirrel.   From time to time I placed my finger near the group of gastronomists ; they all moved away from the banquet at different speeds, indicating different degrees of fear, and always the same insects appearing at each successive alarm.   Only one ant did not deign to pay the slightest attention.

After several attempts I put my finger quite close to the group ; this time they all fled and did not return, with the solitary exception of the one that had not allowed itself to be disturbed.   It quickly turned round, threatening me with its mandibles ; then, lowering its head, it rushed upon me at full speed. I withdrew, overcome by the prodigious moral courage of the insect ! Where would you find a human being with the audacity to withstand a giant taller than the Eiffel Tower ?

True, the insect may be far less conscious of danger than we are ; man injures himself when falling simply his own height on to the ground, whereas the light armour-clad insect may fall from enormous heights without suffering in any way. None the less remarkable was the ant's audacity, especially when we consider that it was purely individual, and not shared by any of its companions.

*　*　*　*　*　*　*

The cat has been most undeservedly calumniated ; men will not forgive him for being proud. They regard it as beneath their dignity to be forced to win the affection of a superior being who is conscious of his worth and lavishes his friendship only where he knows it will be appreciated. No animal could be more cajoling or more faithful than a cat, once you merit his good opinion, but he will not tolerate ill-treatment and he is excessively jealous.

One summer, when I was living in the country, a young tabby from the vicinity had acquired the habit of coming to see me ; she paid me innumerable attentions all the time I was engaged in writing the sombre drama of *Proserpine*. It happened that some one brought along for my inspection a dainty puppy about three months old ; I took it up and kissed it. The cat, seeing this, set up her back and walked angrily away ; it was three days before she returned.

Another time I was living in a small summerhouse, with a number of neighbours all around, similarly housed. There were numerous cats and dogs about, and one, quite a young dog, constituted himself my companion. The animals met every morning in a large court-yard : the dogs played about and gambolled in the happy harmless way with which we are all familiar. The cats took up their quarters on packing-cases from the top of which, in a motionless group, they looked down upon the dogs. No words could do justice to the attitude, at once amused and scornful, with which they contemplated the rough sport and play of the dogs.

A hedge separated me from the next garden : I forbade my little dog to cross it. It was amusing to see what tricks and artifices he employed to baffle

my watchfulness.   He would pretend to be thinking
of something quite different, to be hunting for flies,
then he would suddenly take advantage of a
momentary inattention on my part, whether real or
pretended, and would dart away like an arrow.
During lunch, I seated him on a chair by my side.
If I scolded him for any cause whatsoever, he
assumed an air of melancholy and obstinately
refused the choicest morsels until I had shown, by a
kiss, that he was forgiven.

Let us now imagine ourselves a little farther away,
at Orotava, the pearl of the island of Teneriffe, during one of my winter sojourns in that wonderful
spot.   I had fixed as the goal of my walks a charming botanical garden, rich in curiosities of plant life.
The keeper of the garden had a dog, whose acquaintance I naturally made.   How did that animal come
to understand, one day, that I was paying my last
visit ?

This is a mystery impossible to fathom.   On that
occasion, the dog accompanied me along the road,
a thing which he had never done before.   He would
not leave me.   I drove him away, but he continued
to return.   Some would have thrown stones at him,
but it is not in my nature to adopt this method of
responding to signs of affection.   I did not know
what to do.   Finally, tired of the struggle, I knelt

down by the dog's side, kissed him, and explained
that I could not take him with me, whereupon he
sorrowfully returned home.

* * * * * * *

May I be allowed to say a few words about
Delilah, a black griffon with dark blue eyes which
for ten years has been the delightful companion of
my solitary old age. I will be brief, for one is
inclined to exaggerate regarding the creatures one
has loved ; besides I have no wish to relate what
would be devoid of interest to any one but myself.

She was not more than ordinarily intelligent, but
as she had never been punished, she was very
original and particularly dainty at times. Her
great friend was Lisette, her mother, an excellent
animal whose chief quality was that she was never
troubled with giddiness, a complaint to which dogs
are usually liable. On certain occasions Delilah
was wonderfully attentive to her mother. Neither
of them was given to begging, but whenever it
chanced that they wished to share my dinner,
Delilah allowed Lisette to come forward, taking a
seat behind her at a respectful distance so that her
mother might be served first. Not once did she
fail to do this.

One day, finding a sugar basin uncovered and

K

therefore accessible, Delilah took from it a piece of sugar which she carried to Lisette, afterwards returning for another piece for herself. When Lisette met with a premature death, Delilah almost pined away with grief ; she ceased eating and lost half her weight. This was in the winter time, when I was absent from Paris. On my return—invariably an occasion for joyful barks and gambols which lasted some hours—she had regained somewhat of her former gaiety, though we all felt very uneasy about her. Nothing less than the arrival of a rubber ball, a novelty from London, succeeded in making her forget her trouble and restoring her to health. Her greatest pleasure was to leap on to a table ; she could walk about like a cat and never upset a single one of the fragile ornaments with which it was covered.

On hearing a piano being played she uttered the most piercing cries. Whether she liked or detested it I do not know, for she came running up as soon as the music began instead of running away, though she raised such a series of howls that she had to be carried to the other end of the building as speedily as possible. Neither singing nor the playing of other instruments ever excited her to the same degree.

On the other hand, I once knew a dog which

adored the piano ; as soon as the music began he would come up and crouch beneath the pedals : a matter troublesome enough for the player. To rid oneself of him, all that was necessary was to play Chopin's music. Before eight bars had been played, he had left the room, with dejected ears and his tail between his legs. However often the experiment was tried, the result was invariably the same. Delilah knew the sound of the Eiffel Tower gun ; when it boomed forth, she would make her way to the kitchen for her lunch.

*   *   *   *   *   *   *

I cannot finish without protesting strongly against the useless butcheries practised by so many sportsmen who kill for the pure pleasure of killing. Domestic animals too are also frequently used for wrong purposes.

The more fanatical a nation, the more guilty it is of cruelty to animals. In Europe the Italians and Spaniards are distinguished in this connection, though the Arabs are far worse. In Africa I have witnessed unimaginable horrors, which my pen refuses to describe. Buddha, in teaching metempsychosis to his followers, affords the animal a wonderful degree of protection, whereas Christianity abandons it to any brutality, proclaiming that it is made for man and placing it at his mercy. Never shall I cease bewailing the success that attended the introduction of bull-fights into France : a school of barbarism which makes a pleasure of the sight of death and dishonours the glorious land of Spain.   Little care I what ridicule is poured upon this sentimentality of mine.   The same fate must have befallen those few inhabitants of imperial Rome who took no delight in the circus games, the gladiatorial fights and the lions feasting upon the Christian martyrs.

IMPRESSIONS OF AMERICA

A GREAT many things had been said to me in disfavour of the New World. " America will not please you," they told me, " everything you see will shock your artistic temperament." Pictures had been given me of excited and busy crowds, something like an exasperated England. . . .

Of a certainty, if one expects to feel in America the same emotions as in Rome or Florence, one will be disappointed. In these days, as is well known, tourists go in search of antiquities : old monuments and old pictures. The numbers of archæologists and of connoisseurs in painting throughout the world are amazing ; when I reflect on this, I always picture to myself a young woman I saw in Dresden, standing in front of Raphael's famous Madonna, and gazing intently at the inlaid tiles on the floor ! In the new quarters of Barcelona I discovered architectural masterpieces which I should never tire of admiring, and yet no one ever looks at them. They will, however, a hundred years hence.

As I did not go to America for traces of the past, I was not disappointed at their absence. On the other hand, on reaching New York I admired the beauty of the Hudson, that great river ploughed on every side by enormous multi-decked steamers and spanned by gigantic bridges. The beauty was not of form but of strength and vitality, a beauty of another kind. There is something strange about this city with all its houses which at times resemble towers. There is nothing interesting about some of these giant houses except their fabulous dimensions, though others are worth seeing. Something novel had to be found in the construction of houses : the Americans found it. Certain architects dream of making New York an artistic city : their dream will be realised. They are lavishly profuse with the finest marbles and the costliest wood. At night, when the windows are illuminated to an incredible height and the electric lights are shining all around, the sight is wonderfully fantastic. I may also mention that New York possesses a large and admirable park in which grey squirrels will come right up to your side and beg for nuts.

*   *   *   *   *   *   *

To my mind, nature and the inhabitants form the great attraction of a country. Frequently nature is very beautiful in America to any who can admire it for itself alone : an attitude of mind not usual in travellers.

To many the finest site means nothing unless it is famous and recalls some historic fact. I do not deny that some memorable event may give interest to a landscape, but the Alps would always appear beautiful to me even though they had never been traversed by famous armies.

As regards the inhabitants, I did not find them as they had been depicted to me. Going about at their leisure in spacious streets everywhere, I judged them to be rather quiet compared with the bustling inhabitants of certain towns in the North of France. I found them both courteous and sympathetic. Besides, how could one help being satisfied with a country in which all the women are charming ? And they really are, for those who chance not to be beautiful find it possible to pass themselves off as beautiful. I was afraid I might meet some bachelor women with short hair and harsh expression of face, and was agreeably surprised to find that it was not so. True, in America it is woman who reigns, even a little too much, I am informed ; still, she remains essentially woman and she reigns as she has the right to do, by her charm and grace, her irresistible seductiveness.

To return to art.   Dare I affirm that I frequently found better taste than in certain European cities which I will not mention by name ?   The Americans imitate the Romans, and especially the Greeks, also the fifteenth century and the *Renaissance*.   Is it our place to call them to account for this ?

It seemed to me that their imitations were by no means always maladroit, and that the buildings of Washington, especially those in the Grecian style, were most elegant.   I found bad taste in the theatre and in operettas, where frightful customs— the offspring of Italian operetta, unless I am mis- taken—spoil the lighter type of work, which would otherwise prove acceptable.

New York possesses admirable natural history and other museums which keenly interested me, though I am not competent to speak of them ; also an art museum to describe which would require a volume. Several rooms are given up entirely to the musical instruments of every age and land.

The sculpture is not very imposing, but there are many picture galleries containing brilliant examples of the French school of the nineteenth century. Do not run away with the idea that the Americans have purchased the works of our artists indis- criminately and at too high a price. It is indeed

the pick of the basket that they have acquired.
And, whilst I feel somewhat sad to know that these
artists, with most of whom I was acquainted, have
now passed over, it was a great consolation to know
that they have left behind them so glorious a fame.

Here I saw Rosa Bonheur's *Marché aux chevaux*,
pictures of the highest merit by Meissonier and
Gérome, an admirable Lemercier de Neuville,
dainty portraits of Manet, an exquisite Cazin, two
splendid Desgoffes, Decamps and Isabeys and hosts
of others ! All these paintings have one great
defect : they are not ancient. But wait a little,
that will soon come. To men of my generation the
painter of the eighteenth century was ancient ;
artists of the nineteenth century will be the same
to our children, and I feel no alarm at the place
which the nineteenth century school will occupy in
the eyes of posterity.

Our musical school too makes a good show : in
the second half of the century we have quite a
glorious pleiad dominated by Berlioz the artist,
if not strictly speaking the musician. We have
Reber, so fond of the past, whose somewhat faint
though delicate and finely drawn *gouaches* have
unfortunately been forgotten ; we have the whole
of that brilliant school at the beginning of the
century, the *genre* which was called—at first proudly

though afterwards derisively—*le genre national*, a school somewhat bourgeoise and *terre a terre*, I grant, though so unaffected and gay !

The foreigner, who has done his best to create in us a distaste for all this, the better to inflict his own music on us, continues to be well pleased with himself, and the amateur who crosses the Rhine and dreams of Walhalla and its warrior virgins is quite amazed to see in the streets posters announcing La Dame Blanche, Le Domino Noir, and Le Postillon de Longjumeau.

*   *   *   *   *   *   *

Curiosity holds a large place in the museums of New York. Ancient objects from China and Japan, Oriental porcelain, carved wood, rare and quaint things of every kind abound. The pearl of the collections seems to me to be the jades which fill a whole room. The illustrated catalogues, running to one hundred copies and costing one hundred and fifty thousand francs, are a marvel. One may be seen in Paris, at the library of the Institut.

All this wealth consists of gifts or loans of private individuals who spend fortunes for the purpose of enriching the artistic patrimony of their country. They thus contribute to the education of the nation, which assuredly when it has become homogeneous will also have attained its summit of artistic efflorescence. Even now, Cincinnati, a town with a gentle climate and picturesquely situated, manufactures admirable pottery to which our Expositions have granted awards. You will be surprised also to learn that there is no speculation in all this ; all the profits of the enterprise are devoted to new investigations with a view to ever increasing perfection.

To come to the art in which I am specially interested, I may mention that I found everywhere excellent orchestras, often composed of French performers and led by very good conductors. In New York I was delighted to meet Mr. Walter Damrosch, whose father had taken him there when a child, and with whom Liszt, who thought much of him, had put me in touch just at the time he was preparing to leave Germany for America.

Mr. Damrosch is a worthy successor of his father and is sympathetic to French composers. Nor is he alone in this. Whilst I was in New York, a successful performance of *La Croisade des Enfants* by Gabriel Pierné was given, and in all the towns I visited I found in the repertoire the works of César Franck as well as my own.

In Philadelphia, by a lucky coincidence, a very fine performance of *Samson et Dalila* was given by an amateur company of two hundred and fifty chorists. The *Delila*, both in voice and in talent was perfection itself and in the *Bacchanale* of the last act the orchestra reached the summit of enthusiasm and brilliancy.

I will be brief as to the reception I received personally. Nowhere have I found a more attentive public, more silent and enthusiastic. I had to endeavour to recover my fingering of past days in order to play my Concerto in G Minor which everybody wished to hear interpreted by the composer. This did not please me by any means, for now-a-days young pianists play it better than I do ; I prefer to play the Fifth, which is more symphonic and more fitted to my present powers.

Well then, I played the G Minor at Washington before President Roosevelt who, after receiving me most affably, did me the rare and signal honour of coming to listen to my playing.

Shall I tell how pleased I was to see in Washington the statue of La Fayette along with that of Rochambeau ? The Americans have one quality which touched me greatly, they are not ungrateful : they have not forgotten the part played by France in their independence.

Everywhere one sees statues, busts, portraits, souvenirs and relics of La Fayette. I was delighted with Washington itself, an oasis of verdure where the wide avenues are lined with dainty houses, and where there is neither smoke nor noise, very few trams and twenty-floor sky-scrapers. After all, these high buildings are quite pleasing to dwell in. From such heights, a man feels as though he were floating in a balloon, he becomes intoxicated with space and light. In an electric lift, the top is reached in a few seconds.

In Europe we can form no idea of such comfort. Every hotel bed-room has a bath-room adjoining, and wardrobes large enough to contain trunks and boxes.

Everyone has his own telephone by which he may converse with the whole city all day long if he wishes. Railway journeys—did not frequent accidents act as a sword of Damocles—are far less unpleasant than here. Every ticket bears a number and this number is the one you find disengaged in an immense carriage where you move about as you please without there being any necessity to hurry and bustle to secure a seat. At night, the beds are large and soft, supplied with warm blankets and. quilts. If you like to pay for it, you may have a large cabin capable of accommodating two or even three persons. Steam or hot water circulation ensures a summer temperature in the coldest weather. One consequence of all this is that

Americans move from place to place with the most astonishing ease : I was continually coming across people whom I had seen the previous week six hundred miles away. When meal time comes round, instead of the usual menu you have a choice of varied and excellent dishes served in the most gorgeous fashion and at very moderate prices.

At Detroit I was not a little surprised to find myself in the middle of the water ; the entire train —without any warning having been given—had run on to the steamer and was resuming its journey on the other side of the liquid plain.

*   *   *   *   *   *   *

At the beginning of my stay in New York, I was so ill that my doctor insisted on procuring a nurse for me. I protested, dreading to be handed over to the tender mercies of some ugly frowsy old person. What was my amazement to find myself confronted with a delightful young lady, slender as a reed and fresh as the spring, highly educated, discreet and graceful, neither a prude nor a coquette. The mere sight of her was a comfort and a consolation. She first made her appearance about midnight, wearing a Japanese dressing-gown, to see if the fever had abated and if the doctor's prescriptions were being carried out.

It appears that these charming nurses frequently marry their patients after they have recovered.

At the Metropolitan Opera, *Romeo* is given in French, *Aida* in Italian and *Lohengrin* in German, thus avoiding that treacherous translation which more or less distorts the meaning of an opera and invariably misrepresents its real character. The stage management is not of the best as regards musical execution, and even in *La Traviata* they had suppressed the music on the stage, the original effect of the first act, and the waltz music in the distance which accompanies the dialogue of the two lovers. It may however have been that the suppression was due to some cause independent of the management. . . .

After the play or opera it is the fashion to take supper in the Chinese quarter. These Orientals live some distance away in a few small streets where they have set up restaurants. Here you drink excellent tea and eat " ratatouille," a meat and vegetable stew, which no more resembles the real Chinese cooking—such as I became acquainted with in Saïgon—than does a meal prepared for a Parisian workman in a creamery resemble a dinner at Voisin's or Paillard's. The difference is even greater, for nothing can compare, in point of delicacy, with the true Chinese fare served in fragile tiny painted cups which look as though they had been made for fairies. Sea-weed soups, lotus grains, young bamboo shoots, edible birds' nests, delicious shrimp *pâtes* moulded in the form of flowers and stars, perfumed sauces, small preserved tomatoes, light sticks of tortoise-shell and ivory, spoons of flower-adorned porcelain : the barbarous Occident is unworthy of you !

*   *   *   *   *   *   *

I did not wish to speak of the Zoological Gardens, but I must do so in spite of myself by reason of a pitiful spectacle I saw there—a sight common enough elsewhere, by the way—one that has long haunted my imagination.

I refer to the fact that carnivorous animals are treated unjustly and barbarously under the pretext that they are " ferocious."

Why " ferocious " ?   How is a lion devouring a sheep, an eagle chasing a dove, more ferocious than a stork eating a frog or a swallow an insect ?   In no way.   They are simply formidable to man, and he, the scourge of the animals, will not have it that his victims should attack him in their turn.   The carnivores are treated as criminals.   For herbivores and wading-birds and aquatic fowl generally there is comparative freedom, space and exercise ; for the others, there is close captivity, frequently even deprivation of air and light.

Dens for lions and bears ! In New York I saw foxes and wolves shut up in narrow cages where they could scarcely move. And yet the carnivores include the finest animals in creation ! Would it not be more interesting to see them gambol and sport about than eternally pace to and fro in a prison house ? The lion and the fox are extremely intelligent and are easily tamed. If you gaze upon the former, you cannot help being impressed by that admirable head with its shaggy mane, the profound look in those eyes, and that indefinable air of fallen and resigned majesty. Is it not abominable to condemn this magnificent animal to die of anæmia and consumption ? Make no mistake, I am not now pleading the cause of the animal, I am appealing to man, civilised man, for whom it is disgraceful to act like a savage incapable of reflecting and of understanding nature. Carnivorous animals are dangerous, granted. Then lodge them in such a way that they cannot escape, but do not confine them within a dungeon. The problem is not an insoluble one.

* * * * * * *

Yes, America pleased me well and I would willingly revisit it, but as for living there . . . that

L

is another matter. Born in the early part of the nineteenth century, I belong to the past, whether I like it or not. I shall always prefer our old cities, the sacred relics of Europe, before all the comfort of a young nation. On returning from New York, Paris seemed to me like some pretty *bibelot*, but how glad I was to see it again !

What pleased me abroad was not so much the present America as the idea of what America will eventually be. I seemed to behold a mighty crucible in which a thousand ingredients are mixed to form an unknown substance. In the accomplishment of this task, what an expenditure of activity, wealth and scientific progress in useful and practical—as well as pure—science ! There is one thing especially calculated to astonish : the importance this nation attaches to religious questions ; for, after all, the pursuit of wealth, the lust of domination, the immoderate delight in terrestrial enjoyments are poles asunder from that evangelistic spirit which preaches renunciation, detachment from worldly possessions, humility and disdain of temporal blessings. You wonder less when you reflect that in every age the human soul has been able to reconcile the strangest contradictions. The cruelty of a Louis the Eleventh, the inordinate pride and scandalous life of a Louis the Fourteenth seemed perfectly capable of being reconciled with the loftiest spirit of devotion, and the naïve Madame de Caylus depicts for us as quite natural the *Aigle de Meaux* chatting with the *Roi* in the embrasure of a window and attempting to effect a reconciliation between the King and Madame de Montespan.

Everything one sees in America appears, from a distance, as a kind of mirage, for we are still in a transition period, preparing for a new world. It may be that centuries will be required to give it its perfect form, and meanwhile, who can tell what will have become of this world of ours, carrying the heavy burden of a past which it cannot shake off!

CHOPIN

" CHOPIN ! " When the good King Louis Philippe was alive, you should have heard with what a dainty accent and eager expression women uttered these two syllables. The artiste's elegant manners and the ease with which his name was pronounced certainly contributed largely to the huge success he attained. And besides, he was consumptive at a time when robust health was unfashionable ; women, on sitting down to table, would thrust their gloves into their glass and nibble only a few dainty morsels at the end of a meal. It was considered a mark of *bon ton* for the young to look pale and thin ; Princess Belgiojoso appeared on the Boulevards dressed in black and silver white, looking as wan and ghastly as Death himself.

Chopin's illness, though real enough, was regarded as an attitude he had assumed. This " jeune malade à pas lents," a foreigner with a French name, son of an unhappy country whose fate was pitied and whose resurrection was desired by all in France, was in every way calculated to please the public of the day ; indeed, all this served him better than his musical talent which, as a matter of fact, this same public did not in the least understand.

Proof of this lack of comprehension is to be found in the popularity of a certain Grand Waltz in E Flat, now quite forgotten, but in those days strummed on every piano to the exclusion of other works of Chopin that were really characteristic of his talent. He had but few admirers worthy of the name : Liszt, Ambroise Thomas, Princess Czartoriska, his best pupil, Madame Viardot, George Sand, who extolled him to the skies in her Memoirs, proclaiming him the greatest of composers, " approached by Mozart alone," she added. A childish exaggeration, though at the time a useful counterpoise to the general opinion which saw in Chopin merely an agreeable pianist, and looked upon Liszt as possessed of amazing powers of execution. Thus were judged and interpreted the musical ability of the two geniuses whose influence on the art of music has been so great !

Times have changed. After prolonged years of barren strife, the great compositions of Liszt have taken their rightful place. The Waltz in E Flat is relegated for ever to the store-room, and all the dream-land flowers that appeared in the garden of

the marvellous artiste claimed both by France and
by Poland now blossom in perfect freedom and
scatter their fragrance around. We admire and
love . . . but do we understand . . . them ?

Chopin's musical studies had been so incomplete
that he was forbidden the great vocal and instrumental compositions and had to confine himself to
the piano, wherein he discovered an entirely new
world. This speciality, however, may lead the
judgment astray. When interpreting his works,
we think too much of the piano, of the instrument
regarded as an end in itself ; we forget both
musician and poet. For Chopin is above all a poet
who may be compared with Alfred de Musset : like
the latter he sings of love and women.

More than all else, Chopin was sincere. His
music, without being in accordance with any
particular programme, is invariably a tone picture ;
he did not " make " music, he simply followed his
inspiration. He expresses the most varied human
feelings ; he also gives musical form to the impressions produced in him by the sights of nature. But
whereas in others, in Beethoven, for instance, these
impressions may be pure and unalloyed, in Chopin's
music . . . with the exception of a few polonaises
that voice his patriotism . . . woman is ever present ; everything is referred to her and it is this

standpoint we must adopt if we would give the music its rightful character. His works thrill with a passion . . . now overflowing, now latent or restrained . . . that gives them an inner warmth of feeling which makes them live so intensely, though too frequently this is replaced by an affected and jerky performance, by contortions utterly opposed to his real style, which is both touching and simple.

This latter word may excite surprise when speaking of music that bristles with accidentals, with complicated harmonics and arabesques, but we must not—as is generally done—lay too much stress on these details. Fundamentally the music is simple, it betokens great simplicity of heart, and it is this that must be expressed when we play it, under penalty of completely falsifying the intentions of the composer.

Chopin distrusted himself : he invited . . . and sometimes followed . . . pernicious advice, unaware that he himself, guided by instinctive genius, was more clear-sighted than all the savants around him, who were devoid of genius of any kind.

At the beginning of the famous Ballade in G Minor, in the last bar of the introduction, we find in the original edition that a D had manifestly been written down, though subsequently it was corrected into an E. This supposed E gives an expression of pain, quite in harmony with the character of the *morceau*. Was this a printer's error ? Was it the original intention of the composer ? The note produces a dissonance, with unexpected effect. Now, dissonances were at that time dreaded, though nowadays as welcome as truffles. From Liszt, whom I questioned on the matter, I could obtain nothing except that he preferred the E Flat. So do I, but that is not the point. The conclusion at which I have arrived is that Chopin, when playing the Ballade, sounded the D, but I am still convinced that the E Flat was his first inspiration and that the D was adopted on the advice of timid and maladroit friends.

These marvellous works are threatened with a great peril. Under pretext of popularising them, there have appeared new editions, bristling with erroneous fingering. That indeed in itself would be a small matter, but alas ! they have also been improved upon—" perfectionnées "—and this means that alien intentions may gradually replace those of the composer himself.

I cannot enter into the technical details necessitated by such an enquiry, but it is high time some one thought of bringing out an edition, if not of all his works, at least of those that deserve to be handed down to posterity, going back to the fountain head and shewing us the master's thought in all its purity. This fountain head consists of manuscripts, wherever they can be found, original editions, now very rare, Tellefsen's edition, at present difficult to find, badly engraved and printed, and containing many faults, though these are easy to see and can be corrected. Before it is too late, may a really intelligent editor raise to Chopin's memory this imperishable monument that has nothing in common with the *Kritik-Ausgaben* with which the musical world is invaded as by some destructive phylloxera !

CHARLES GOUNOD ON MOZART'S
" DON JUAN "

Is it simply the memory of a dream when I see myself, in those far-away days of my sixth year, gravely accompanying a beautiful *cantatrice* as she sings a romance I had composed for her ? I had written it down in pencil, the whole of it, and my great-aunt, who was also my god-mother and my music teacher—a lady belonging to an aristocratic family ruined by the Revolution, through which she herself had passed—had piously gone over it in ink. Naturally, at that age, I would never have tolerated anyone giving me the slightest help in the composition ! The masterpiece was twelve bars in length, four of them consisting of a *ritornelle*. Such as it was, it had astonished the singer's father, an old soldier who was very fond of music ; the result being that he presented me with the orchestral score, in two handsome red volumes, of Mozart's *Don Juan*, with French and Italian text.

When I think of it, such a present to so young a child appears somewhat audacious ; assuredly

very few would have made it. All the same, the
donor could not have been better inspired. Daily
in my *Don Juan*, unconsciously though with that
wonderful ease of assimilation which is the great
characteristic of childhood, I lived in the music,
reading the score and acquainting myself with both
the vocal and the instrumental parts. What a
delight it was, some years later, to listen to this
opera at the Italiens, sung by Grisi, Mario, and
Lablache ; and when, later still, being intimate
with Gounod, I had the pleasure of hearing him
interpret and comment on the work, every page
of which I knew by heart !

No wonder, then, that I discovered nothing very
new to me on opening Gounod's book on Mozart's
masterpiece. Still, how few readers would find
themselves in so exceptional a situation ? Not one.
I will even add that most of those who think they
know *Don Juan*, from having gone through it
rapidly or heard it at the Opéra, split up into five
Acts, spoiled by the translation and the sacrilegious
alterations, even additions, of Castil-Blaze, in that
vast building so unsuited both to the dainty orchestral music and to the subject-matter, are in reality
completely ignorant of it. Consequently, I make
one request of those interested in music : to forget
for the time being their usual preferences and

transcendental theories, and, instead, read this
short though substantial book, so attractive and
yet profound beneath its apparent slightness. They
will learn much of which they had previously no
idea, and the reading will enable them to see that
in art there is something more precious than con-
viction, viz., artistic probity—that quality inherent
in the fine works of the past—surrounding *Don
Juan* with a scared halo, and which Gounod, in his
panegyric of the masterpiece, brings out so
brilliantly.

Let us open the famous score. At once we are
conscious that the criticism is of a superior kind :

> From the beginning of the Overture Mozart
> flings himself completely into the spirit of the
> drama, the Overture itself being an epitome of
> it. After the first four bars, rendered yet more
> terrible by the pause which completes the second
> and fourth . . . .

It is unusual to attach such importance to pauses,
a thing calculated to astonish many, for the eloquence of the pause in music is a comparatively
modern conquest. Whether we take the Roman
style of Palestrina or the monumental artistry of
Bach, the whole past art has entirely, or almost
entirely, misinterpreted it. Nowadays we appear

to scorn this valuable aid, preoccupied as we are
with stretching too tightly the warp and woof of
the musical fabric and covering it with rich em-
broidery. All the same, the effect of the pause is one
of rare potency which nothing else can supply. To
such as would think slightingly of Mozart, I recommend the pauses that interrupt the first few bars
of the Prelude of *Tristan*. Let them endeavour
to suppress these in thought, and they will discover how important they are.

To continue :

Everything in this tremendous introduction
breathes and inspires terror : the monotonous
and inexorable rhythm of the strings, the sepul-
chral timbre of the wind instruments, where the
octave intervals, from bar to bar, resemble the
very trampings of a stone giant, the minister of
Death ; the syncopations of the first violins
which, from the eleventh bar onwards, probe
the innermost recesses of that sombre conscious-
ness, the creation of the second violins entwining
like a huge reptile round the culprit, the stubborn
resistance of this condemned victim who blindly
struggles on to the end ; those frightful scales,
ascending and descending, which swell like the
billows of a stormy sea ; in a word, the menace

suspended over the head of the criminal by
the solemnity of so impressive an opening; everything in this wonderful page is of the loftiest
tragical inspiration ; the power of fearsome
terror could go no further.

This picture is a true one, and yet, on close
inspection, how paltry the details seem ! Mere
octave intervals, basses representing a very simple
rhythm for a few bars, syncopations—where do
we not find these ? A trifling arrangement on the
fourth string of the second violins, and those scales,
ces effroyables gammes, moderate in *tempo* and not
more than one octave in range : can such things
be wonderful ? It is true that the details of themselves appear little or nothing, they acquire all
their importance from being timely or appropriate,
from their reciprocal harmonies, their contrasts,
and a sense of general balance. Here is style ;
here is the secret of genius. It may be invented,
studied, and analysed, though with great difficulty ;
it cannot be imitated. It also disappears in ordin-
ary average playing ; a piece of music may be
played quite well, to all appearance, and yet produce no impression whatsoever.

Nothing, unfortunately, is more difficult to
interpret than this exquisite music whose every

note and pause has a value of its own and where
the slightest negligence, whether in letter or in
spirit, may be catastrophic.   Great musical
spectacles have a virility of another kind ; the
Overture of *Tannhaüser*, that of *Guillaume Tell*—
for I have no preconceived ideas on the matter—
survive second-rate interpretations ;   however one
murders the notes, there are so many of them that
there are always some to spare.   This constitutes
the triumph of the big guns !   The tree with its
thousands of leaves may weather the storm, but
what is left of a flower—of a butterfly's wing—
once it has been bruised or crushed ?

* * * * * * *

The drama begins.   In vivid colours the author
has depicted the famous Introduction where,
epitomised, so to speak, so many apparent incon-
gruities easily find room :   the comic scene of
Leporello awaiting his master, the flight of Don
Juan stopped by Donna Anna, the appearance of
the Commander, the duel and its fatal issue.   Attention might have been drawn to the extraordinary
facility with which, at each step, Mozart modifies
the character of the music, passing from comic to
tragic without breaking the unity of style.   I have
purposely used the word " facility " instead of

" skill " since it is very likely that the miracle was effected unconsciously. In this scene, as in that of the supper which concludes the opera, Mozart certainly realised the impossible without being aware of the fact. The musical language he used, consisting of a happily proportioned blend of the Italian and the German style, sustained by universally accepted tradition, was extremely supple, though how many, employing the same medium of expression, lack his eloquence !

The minutely detailed analysis of the well-known air of Leporello, *Madamina, il catalogo è questo*, is particularly to be noted. When we find Gounod seeking meanings and intentions in each note, we might conclude that he had given free scope to his imagination. Nothing of the kind ; everything he says is true, and yet the *morceau* flows smoothly along, each detail appearing to be required by musical necessities alone. Here is the difficulty in the ever-recurring question of music with literary pretensions ; on condition the style does not suffer, we may put into music as many intentions as we please. Those who do not like them need not notice them.

With regard to this air and the eloquent details of its instrumentation, Gounod remarks :

Here we have the orchestra in the theatre filling its proper rôle, which is complementary rather than invading, not saying too much, and yet saying all. How far removed we are from dull, pretentious pomposity which aims at moving us by loud effects, which looks upon mere padding as real worth and upon pathos as greatness !

In these words we have the clash of weapons before the battle ; but the fight does not come on, the author not considering it necessary to insist on his point. Apparently the artistic epoch in which Mozart lived, analogous to our 17th century French literature, enters largely into the qualities Gounod admires—true balance and perfection of taste. He is quite right to protest against *striving after effect ;* the absence of such striving is common to all fine periods in art, its presence is a characteristic sign of decadence.

I am greatly inclined to find fault with the unguarded encomiums Gounod lavishes on Don Juan's "Ball," with his three orchestras on the stage, each, as we know, playing a different air. "All this," he says, "is carried through *without confusion,* but with consummate ease and skill."

That may be true when reading the opera, but

M

when listening to this portion of it I have always
been quite bewildered.   The sun may have spots
on its surface : Gounod cannot see them.   But
though I see the spot, I do not find fault with the
author ; I merely declare that I do not understand
what he meant.   Considering that during the
supper of the second Act he introduced wind instruments on to the stage, he might also have introduced
some during the Ball instead of increasing the
numbers of violins and basses, the result of which
was an inextricable jumble of instruments of like
timbre.   What reasons had he for doing so ?
Probably under his interpretation the *morceau*
assumed a different meaning from that which
it has for us.   In any case there is but one thing
for us to do : play the piece just as it is written.

Nothing is more dangerous than to make alterations in such a work.   I remember, on the occasion
of a reprise of *Don Juan* at the Opéra, Vaucorbeil,
who was then director, was astonished at the lack
of effect produced by the famous Trio of Masks.
As is well known, this Trio is preceded by a conversation between the three Masks, in admirably
tragic vein.   A window opens, the orchestra suddenly stops, and through the open window are
wafted strains of the small orchestra of the Ball,
accompanying Leporello's invitation.   When the

window is shut, the orchestra resumes and the admirable Trio begins. On the occasion of the reprise in question, the small stage orchestra had been suppressed and the theatre orchestra played everything itself, with the result that the entire picturesque passage became impossible to understand and most pitifully commonplace.

The instrumentation of the magnificent air of Donna Anna, *Or sai chi l'onore*, contains another puzzle. Gounod makes no mention of it whatsoever, he even praises the full, sonorous orchestra " which never goes beyond what is necessary." I am not wholly of this opinion. In this *morceau*, where the vocal part shows such grandeur and spirit, my opinion is that the orchestra does not attain " what is necessary." Berlioz was fond of ridiculing it. Doubtless, after the grandiose singing of Donna Anna, oboes and bassoons seem inadequate, almost comical. The puzzle may be solved by supposing that the singer who created the rôle may have been vocally unequal to the occasion. Mozart was always very careful not to drown the singing beneath heavy instrumentation ; he might be called a voice-setter just as a jeweller might be called a diamond-setter.

So far I have been rather, perhaps even immoderately, abusive towards Gounod, so it is time I began

praising and admiring him again. I will not undertake to make a list of his sayings, his *trouvailles*,
the pearls in his casket. Open it ; you will be
surprised and dazzled. Listen to what he says of
the famous balcony Trio :

> It is in the very phrases of Donna Elvira that
> Don Juan seeks the insolent expression of a false
> tenderness. This borrowing is an abuse of con-
> fidence, a musical forgery perpetrated by Don
> Juan, speaking with his own lips the very language
> of sincerity uttered by his wife, the better to
> deceive her.

Is not this way of speaking music both delightful and unexpected ? In another place, he talks
of the "involuntary scruples with which the dis-
interested innocence of genius swarms." We are
continually receiving flashes of light, opening up
hitherto unknown depths, well calculated to amaze
those who seek in music nothing but vague sensations and drugged voluptuousness.

Read this little book, more especially the appen-
dix, in which, leaving his subject, the author deals
with general matters in a few clear-cut sentences.
Reflect on what he says of singing and diction, of
pronunciation and style, learning from him what
the conductor of an orchestra ought to be. Among
other things he says :

It is a mistake to think that the conductor can make himself fully understood by means of the baton which he holds in his hand. His entire demeanour must instruct and impart life to those who obey him. His attitude, his physiognomy, his glance, should prepare the singers for what he is about to demand of them ; his expression should enable them to anticipate his intentions ; it should guide the intelligence of the performers.

How few conductors reach this standard ! For one worthy of the name, how many time-beaters ! Some look as though they were cutting up a cake, others leading a regiment to the drill-ground, others again might be engaged in the hurried preparation of an omelette. I have even seen some twirling the baton above their heads ! The public sets up a claim to judge of the merits of conductors, a disastrous claim which has frequently brought bad musicians to the front because they happened to have cultivated a leonine head of hair or an elegant figure, or simply because they had established a bond of sympathy with the listeners, without the latter really knowing why ! Composers and performers are alone capable of judging in such matters. The chief quality of a conductor, apart from a thorough acquaintance with the work, should be, as Gounod says, a power of suggestion, of such a nature as to elicit from the performer an obedience of which he is not aware. These, as everyone will agree, are matters with which the public has nothing to do ; still, the public likes to judge everything, and its tastes are at times odd enough—especially in music. Formerly it expected music to be of a rousing nature ; now it wants to be lulled to sleep. What will it expect music to do next ?

The noble Muse is little concerned with all this ; all she cares for is to remain beautiful and to lavish smiles on her elect. These are few, as they have always been and probably always will be. " What a lot of notes ! " was said in complimentary tones to Mozart by the Emperor of Austria, who had understood nothing of the wonderful music to which he had been listening. " Sire, there is not one too many," replied Mozart, with a pride equal to his genius.

So great a character but seldom attains to fortune : the author of *Don Juan* died in poverty, to the everlasting shame of his contemporaries.

THE ORIGIN OF
" SAMSON AND DELILAH "

SOME years ago, an old melomaniac who was
in the habit of visiting me called my attention
to the subject of Samson, with a view to the
production of an oratorio—a form of music which
at the time was in considerable favour. Owing
to modern progress, this is a form which can no
longer be utilised. . . . Nowadays we have only
orchestral concerts. An exception is made in the
case of *La Damnation de Faust* because of its
assured financial success.

I had recently made a charming acquaintance,
Fernand Lemaire, an amateur poet, who was
connected with my family by marriage. Some of
his poems I had set to music, and I now suggested
to him the writing of an oratorio. " An oratorio ! "
he replied, " no, let it be an opera " And we
decided for an opera. No sooner did the matter
get abroad, however, than there was a general
outcry of protest. A Biblical opera ! All the
same, though legendary opera was in fashion, I

did not allow myself to become discouraged. My poet had written the first two Acts ; I also had scribbled a few notes—legible to myself alone— of the first Act and the whole of the second. Nevertheless—almost incredible to relate—apart from the sketch of the Prelude, the opera existed only in my head, and wishing to give a few friends some idea of it at my home, I wrote down the music of the three rôles, without a note of the orchestral score.

I have forgotten the names of the three singers whom, naturally, I accompanied from memory, seeing that, with the exception of the vocal parts, nothing whatever had been committed to writing.

The audience, small though specially chosen— Anton Rubinstein being of the number—sat there in stony silence. The composer received not the faintest acknowledgment, even of mere politeness.

A little later the same two Acts were played at my house by Augusta Holmès, Henri Regnault— a very good singer possessed of a delightful tenor voice—and Romain Bussine. The result was a little more satisfactory, though so slightly encouraging that I finally decided to do nothing further with so chimerical a work.

Years passed . . .

One day, in Germany, where I had gone to take

part in a series of musical festivals presided over by Liszt, just as I was on the point of returning to France and was bidding the great pianist farewell, the idea came into my head to mention the matter to him. " Finish your opera," he said to me (though he had not heard a single note of it), and I will produce it for you." As everyone well knows, Liszt was omnipotent at Weimar.

About that time Madame Viardot was in splendid voice, and had given the most brilliant performances at Weimar. It was for her that the part of Delilah was created. At Croissy, on a society stage set up in a garden, she went through half the second Act, along with Nicot and Romain Bussine. The director of the Opéra and a few other Parisians were present : the result was nil. There was no orchestra : only myself accompanying on a grand pianoforte.

Finally the time came to produce the work at Weimar. The translation had been made . . . but the war of 1870 put a stop to everything. It was not till December, 1873, that *Samson and Delilah* saw the footlights ; though, alas ! without the collaboration of Madame Viardot. It was too late.

The success was great, though not sustained. At Berlin it was alleged that the Weimar success had no meaning or significance whatsoever. It was sung at Hamburg, and that was all.

Only after a period of ten years was the opera given in France, at Rouen. Paris would have nothing to do with it. M. Ritt had to hear it at the Eden before he would bring himself to produce it at the Opéra, during the year of the great eruption of Etna. And I had to travel from Paris to Etna and back to witness both the eruption and the first rehearsal of *Samson!*

For the storm in the second Act I had been promised the most wonderful *mise en scène*. Meanwhile, it had been decided to stage the *Walküre* immediately afterwards, and all the promises made to me were broken. I actually had to protest violently before I could obtain for the beginning of the second Act a dash of red to represent the twilight!

MODERN MUSIC

A SPEECH delivered at Fontainebleau on the inauguration of the École des Hautes Études Musicales, 26th
June, 1921.

OF all the arts, the one which captivates the
soul most completely and penetrates most deeply
into the heart of man is Music. In founding this
School, it has been the main purpose of Messieurs
Fragnaud and Casadesus to strengthen the bonds
which link together France, guardian of past
traditions, and America, the land of the
future : France, once the land which eman-
cipated America, and America set free by France.
I have seen for myself that America is not forgetful
of her liberators. At the San-Francisco Exposition, also, I saw what gigantic steps she had
taken in all the arts, and how intensely interested
she was in music. There, in a vast hall provided
with a magnificent organ, various orchestras gave
admirable concerts before a most attentive and
enthusiastic public.

Up to the present, there has been a tendency among young American musicians to go for their training and instruction to Germany, attracted by the renown of the great and glorious masters she has given to the world. It is a mistake, however, to attribute the entire merit to Germany; we are too readily disposed to forget that the modern musical world had its beginnings in Italy. Though the great German masters, dazzling us by their genius, have momentarily blinded us to this truth, on calm reflection we find that even such a genius as Bach, who appears to be Germanic in his very essence, was considerably influenced by Italian music. Later on, the influence of France began to be felt, and from a happy blend of the Italian, the German and the French temperament, came into being that admirable school of music which is German only in name but in reality belongs to the whole world.

Mozart himself was not a German; he was a native of the Tyrol, and so half Italian. Because he spoke ill of her in his letters, it has been said that he did not love France; certainly he met with difficulties and disappointments in France; also his mother died there. All the same, he went to Molière for the subject matter of his

Don Juan and to Beaumarchais for the whole of the *Mariage de Figaro*. Gluck, too, though German by birth, was Italian for the greater part of his life, finally becoming French in his latter years, the most brilliant portion of his career.

In the case of Meyerbeer we find the same blending of nationalities and the same culmination.

Thus we see that music, far from having no *patrie* at all, actually had three during its most glorious epoch. Let us hope it will have four when America, ever becoming greater in art as in science, shall have added her own distinctive and personal metal to the precious alloy.

Above all, let the young avoid all straining after originality. Allow your personal contribution to music to express itself naturally. By eagerly desiring to be original, the result is very likely to be a blend of folly and *bizarrerie*. An instance of such madness is seen in the Italian architects of the twelfth century, who, in their eagerness to break away from the banality of the vertical, constructed those leaning towers which disfigure the city of Bologna.

At this very moment the entire world of music is suffering from a like disease : a craving for novelty at any cost. There are people now living who proclaim aloud their right to become a law unto themselves. Persons knowing nothing either of grammar or of orthography, a law unto themselves ! We know what the result will be.

Primitive music consisted of two elements alone : melody and rhythm. The musical art, strictly so called, began when an attempt at polyphony was made. The first results were rude and barbarous, consisting of successions of fourths and fifths. Then, in a desire to produce simultaneously several independent parts, nothing but cacophony came of it.

Afterwards, very strict rules were instituted, resulting in that magnificent school of the sixteenth century. Here the priestly music was either wholly or almost inexpressive, though its disciples were passionately devoted to it, seeing that they had ceased to find interest in any but learned combinations of sounds, melody being relegated to the sphere of song or dance tunes.

Finally the rules were made more elastic, less strict ; music became more expressive and simple, and strictly scientific music gave place to the various embellishments of song. Forbidden chords were permitted ; the most audacious dissonances gradually found their way into the music of the times, until we reached the position in which we now find ourselves.

We even note a desire to continue farther along the same path, but that is impossible ; the extreme limit has been reached. To go beyond would mean a relapse into the cacophony from which we have emerged.

Besides, there is no need for it. In the vast field of present-day music there is plenty of room for inventions which, though not mathematically, are practically endless. Innovations do not necessarily mean that we must have recourse to dissonance, though this still continues ; we pile tonality upon tonality under the pretext that people can get accustomed to anything.

I have a neighbour who makes painful efforts to play the piano. This instrument has remained untuned ever since the world began ; the pitch of the upper octaves is a half-tone below the middle keys. The lady, however, does not appear to be aware that anything is wrong, seeing that she makes no attempt to remedy the existing state of things.

One can become accustomed to uncleanliness, to vice, even to crime. There are people in the world to whom robbery or assassination are matters of habit. Why cannot we understand that in art, as in everything else, there are some things to which we must not accustom ourselves !

Some would like to make a *tabula rasa*, a clean sweep of everything and owe no debt of any kind to the past. But we do not keep a tree alive by hacking away at the roots.

There are fashions in music as in millinery, and for some time past it has been the fashion to decry the brilliant school of light music which, after giving us Méhul, Dalayrac, Boieldieu, Auber and his successors, has brought to birth those two works of genius : *Carmen* and *Manon*. This school has had its weak points ; it has also been the charm and delight of successive generations. Such works as *La Dame Blanche*, *Le Pré aux Clercs*, *Le Domino Noir*, *Galathée*, *Mignon*, to quote no others, are anything but negligible ; they have their place in the history of music as Marivaux and Regnard by the side of Corneille and Molière in the history of literature.

Another fashion is that which banishes from the art of singing everything in the nature of *vocalises* and *fioriture* or other melodic embellishments, whereas we ought to express amazement that two small ligaments, the vocal cords, are capable of producing such effects. Until quite recently these artifices had been used by all the Italian, German and French composers. Berlioz was the first to throw ridicule upon those singers who " jouaient du larynx "; then came Richard Wagner who retained only the trill or shake, He would even have liked to suppress the art of singing altogether, for did he not proclaim that melody should be entrusted to the orchestra, not to the voice, as though the human voice were not itself the finest of all instruments! It must be noted that the reason some of his works have become very successful is that he frequently forgot to apply this this principle to them himself.

From the Opéra-Comique was born a daughter who turned out badly, so to speak : the operetta. But then, daughters who turn out badly are not always devoid of some good qualities, and the operetta, with all its faults, has retained the dialogue, thus compelling the actors really to act and to articulate. This they do when singing, whereas singers who do nothing but sing too frequently neglect to act the part and to articulate the words ; the listener cannot distinguish one from the other, and the work becomes incomprehensible. -

And now I must stop. France welcomes you and gladly sees the gifted youth of to-day, who come to her for instruction, answer her call. Let

N

us have faith in the future.   The close and intimate
union of France and America will ensure the
triumph of Peace without which the arts could
never flourish.

GOUNOD

(A short discourse intended for the inauguration of the monument erected to the memory of Gounod in the Parc Monceau, Paris. This speech was not delivered).

If anything could console us for the loss of our beloved master, it would be the contemplation of this living marble wherein the features of an artiste of genius appear before us in a medium fit for gods and heroes ; the chisel of an eminent sculptor bringing before us a great musician ; art adding additional comeliness to a face which none who had once seen it could ever forget. But who will give back expression to those eyes, so frank, so intelligent and so good-natured ? Who will restore the smile, the enchanting voice, the familiar talk every sentence of which was a lesson, each word sparkling like a diamond. Time, in thy implacable flight, of what rich stores hast thou robbed us, a treasure that nothing can replace !

A strange career was that of Gounod ! Opposed from the very outset, as all creators are, courageously steering his course against wind and tide, it was his destiny never to know the peace of unchallenged success and tranquil glory ; it was amid storms but seldom interrupted by brief spells of calm weather that he became the most popular musician in France.

Pre-eminently was he a creator. Only in part are Marguérite, Juliette and Mireille the offspring of Goethe, Shakespeare and Mistral ; the musician as well as the poet gives birth to children of his own, creations less complete, it may be, though nearer to the masses and possessed of that gift of ubiquity which it is the nature of music to bestow. England alone fully understands the Juliet of Shakespeare, Germany the Gretchen of Goethe, and Provence the Mireille of Mistral, but the public of the civilised world regard Marguérite, Mireille and Juliette as the daughters of Gounod. Less complex in nature than the children of the poets and animated by an intense musical life, they form part and parcel of our daily portion and receive us into their intimacy. Stripped of their precious garments they lay bare their heart's emotions, thrilling us in accord with their most secret and hidden feelings and leaving for their illustrious sisters the shining ornaments of the mind. Listen to Marguérite as she sings :

. . . Ceux dont la main cruelle me repousse
N'ont pas fermé pour moi la porte du saint lieu ;
J'y vais pour mon enfant et, pour lui, prier Dieu.

Listen to the simple chord that accompanies
these last few words, thrilling us with a grief for
which no consolation can ever be found, affording
us a glimpse of the disturbing and mysterious
depths of the vast cathedral, and then tell me if
any other art can attain to such results with so few
means and appliances !

Does not the cathedral in " Faust " seem a kind
of link between the dramatic author and the
chorister, symbolised by the organ which is shown
on the stage ? The religious music of Gounod is
great, more especially the Mass of Saint Cecilia and
the Requiem of " Mors et Vita," the Mass written
at the beginning, and the Requiem at the end of
his career, the former adorned with all the bright-
ness of a glorious dawn, the latter burning with the
golden fires of a setting sun. In them we find
sincerity of faith wedded to perfection of form, to a
power and quality of voice that daily become more
rare before the jealous and domineering influx of
instrumental music. And yet, is it not the human
voice that is the one living and divine instrument ?
To those who have loved and served the voice, not
in its errors but in its triumphant beauty, it gives
as a reward the palm of immortality. Instruments
change and pass into oblivion ; the voice remains.
Still may we sing Palestrina, Roland de Lassus and

Jennequin ; it would be impossible to resurrect the instrumental music of the sixteenth century whose wonderful organs and lutes are now no more than dainty *bibelots* relegated to private collections and public museums.

Illustrious master ! thou hast shown us the path to follow, guiding and encouraging when the way was dark and uncertain ; thou hast overthrown the difficulties and obstacles and we have had but to continue resolutely along the road opened out for us through storm and stress.   Thanks be to thee and glory *in eternum !*